The American New Wave
1958-1967

Walker Art Center
Media Study / Buffalo

During the past few years, a good deal of attention has been focused on the efforts of independent filmmakers to reach large audiences while maintaining a significant degree of artistic control and independence. This growing commitment to a viable independent film practice carries with it the conviction that there exists a diversity of artistic options beyond those offered by Hollywood and commercial television. One of the reasons for organizing *The American New Wave: 1958–1967* had to do with this renewed interest in independent feature filmmaking and an awareness, on our part, that there had already been a series of attempts, begun in the late 50s, to place film in the hands of individual artists. A retrospective examination of this earlier period, we hoped, would provide a more adequate picture than conventional history affords us of a rare period of American cinematic invention and thereby prepare a coherent critical and historical context for the reception of new work by the current generation of independent filmmakers.

The emergence of this first American independent cinema parallelled stylistic developments and movements in other countries—in particular, the new waves of France and Poland and the Free Cinema of Britain. All these "waves" had in common an ambition to declare their independence from traditional studio production values, to challenge the economic structures of the film industry, and to make films that would reflect a contemporary reality rendered invisible by the studio film. But while the European counterparts of this movement, and the French New Wave, in particular, have been well documented and analyzed, the American films of the same period have lapsed into relative and undeserved obscurity—a somewhat surprising development since virtually all of the films included in this retrospective enjoyed a strong critical reception both here and abroad at the time of their original release. Many of the films received enthusiastic reviews in mainstream publications like *The New York Times;* Lionel Rogosin's *Come Back, Africa* was included as one of the ten best films of 1960 by *Time* magazine; a number of the films obtained theatrical distribution or were premiered at major film festivals; in France, several of the screenplays were published and an entire volume was devoted to a critical assessment of the work. And yet today, particularly in this country, very little of this history is preserved.

We chose to begin this retrospective in 1958 for historical reasons. 1958—when Lionel Rogosin was making *Come Back, Africa;* Robert Frank and Alfred Leslie, *Pull My Daisy;* John Cassavetes, *Shadows;* and Sidney Meyers, Joseph Strick and Ben Maddow, *The Savage Eye*—saw the flowering of independent filmmaking in America. This movement, at first, included an array of dramatic, documentary and experimental filmmakers united, as Jonas Mekas wrote in *Film Culture* in 1959, by their opposition to the "official cinema" of the "Hollywoods all over the world." Hollywood films, according to this "Call for a New Generation of Filmmakers," were "made with money, cameras, and splicers, instead of with enthusiasm, passion and imagination. . . . Our hope for a free American cinema is entirely in the hands of the new generation of filmmakers. And there is no other way of breaking the frozen cinematic ground than through a *complete* derangement of the official cinematic senses."

The "derangement," though perhaps not complete, was far-reaching. The filmmakers shared with the beat writers, abstract expressionist painters and jazz musicians of the 50s and early 60s a desperate need to combat the complacency of middle-class America, the racial inequalities of its social systems, and the dispiriting academic idea of an intellectual and artistic elite. What was important to them was to record the reality of the present moment in its raw, spontaneous state. They wanted to break down the barriers between life and art or, as the New American Cinema Group expressed it in their "First Statement" published in *Film Culture* (Summer 1961): " . . . we are for art, but not at the expense of life. We don't want false, polished, slick films—we prefer them rough, unpolished, but alive; we don't want rosy films—we want them the color of blood."

One of the truly unique aspects of this movement was perhaps its willingness to make aesthetic and stylistic virtues out of economic limitations. In rejecting elaborate studio sets and lighting for real location shooting and available light, movie stars for unknown actors or non-professionals, large crews for small, and, in some cases, synchronized sound for freedom in shooting and editing, the filmmakers were accommodating their own limited financial resources. At the same time, the economic necessities themselves were a function of the desire to make films from life and to reflect upon contemporary social realities by concentrating on the everyday. This meant that they relied on the actors, the locations and events to determine dialogue and story structure and thus fulfilled a direction in filmmaking formulated a decade earlier by the film critic James Agee as quoted by Jonas Mekas in *Film Culture* (Spring 1962), "The films I most eagerly look forward to will not be documentaries but works of fiction, played against and into and in collaboration with unrehearsed and uninvented reality." It is this unrehearsed quality and the

engagement with the cultural and political realities of the disenfranchised, be it poet or black teenager, that give these films their vitality.

In selecting the films for this retrospective, we were first of all interested in highlighting the early developments of American independent feature filmmaking. This meant including not only filmmakers who are easily identified with the New American Cinema Group, but also some like Michael Roemer, Robert Young, George Kuchar, Robert Downey and Jim McBride who are not. In addition, we wanted to program the films in such a way as to raise important aesthetic, stylistic and ethical questions useful for contemporary filmmakers and audiences. The most compelling of these issues seemed to be ideas about reality as reflected in the combination of fictional and documentary elements, performance and acting, and camera and editing style. A sense of the period was also important. And although there are exceptions, we were especially interested in films that aspired to some sort of theatrical release and in films produced by those who continued to work in the medium.

While the main focus of this retrospective is the narrative feature, some of the films were selected for other reasons that are exceptions: *Portrait of Jason* and *The Brig,* for example, are documentaries, but each address ethical and aesthetic issues about film and reality in a way that makes them pertinent to this series. *Hold Me While I'm Naked* is a narrative work but not a feature. However, we felt that Kuchar's usurpation of and comment on Hollywood techniques were so to the point that we had to represent him by his greatest film.

This catalogue is divided into three sections. The first consists of personal accounts of the period by

three major figures within it: Jonas Mekas, Shirley Clarke and Taylor Mead. Mekas as filmmaker, founder and editor of *Film Culture* from 1955 to the present, and as film critic of *The Village Voice* from 1958 to 1975 is perhaps the single most accurate critic and consistent chronicler of this period and is represented here by excerpts from his diaries. Shirley Clarke as a driving force behind the independent feature film movement is interviewed by Melinda Ward. Taylor Mead who appeared in many underground films and off-off Broadway theater productions discusses his career as an actor during this perid. The second section includes essays especially commissioned for this catalogue. The third section is informational and includes film credits, filmographies, a bibliography and a chronology of the period.

In assembling the retrospective program, preparing this catalogue and organizing the touring exhibition, we have received support and advice from many individuals. We would especially like to thank Jonas Mekas for his excellent counsel. Our thanks as well to Virgil Grillo, Leo Dratfield, Larry Kardish, Blaine Allen, Leslie Trumbull, Robert Fieldsteel, David Shepard, Nancy Sher and Tony Safford. We would like to thank The Sundance Institute and Sterling Van Wagonen, Executive Director for sponsoring the opening of the tour with a three-day symposium at the U.S. Film and Video Festival in Park City, Utah, January 1983. And, finally, we wish to acknowledge the special support given by one of the first advisors to this project, independent filmmaker James Blue. This catalogue is dedicated to his memory.

Melinda Ward
Director of Media
Walker Art Center

Bruce Jenkins
Film Programmer
Media Study/Buffalo

From the Diaries

Jonas Mekas

---

10 December 1954

Still looking for money. Last week our books showed that we have only $120. The sum needed to pay for the next issue of *Film Culture* is $700. During last few days I've approached at least thirty people, in film business, for sponsorship. I got mostly the names but no money.

While preparing the first issue, I was mostly concentrating on the contents. Money seemed such a secondary thing. But now I am facing the reality.

I reported on the sad financial situation to the Editorial Board. I simply proposed that each of us come up with $100—and the problem is solved! The idea didn't work. F. is going to South America and has not a single dollar left. B. said he is willing to give any help to the magazine except the financial help. H. said he has money but he wouldn't give because of his principles. Why, he said, why did you start the magazine at all, without money! You can't start a magazine unless you have money at least for three or four issues, he said. If he'd known that we don't have money he wouldn't have helped from the beginning. So I said, if we'd all think that way, *Film Culture* would wait for another two centuries. There are thousands of people with money and business brains, but it had to be us, without money and without business brains, to do the job. Gods are cruel . . . I didn't dare to tell him that this morning we received summons to appear in court. Pacific Printing is suing us for the printing of the first issue of *Film Culture*. We have seven days to pay $723.91.

11 December 1954

I am continuing the money odyssey. Perry Miller said she spent all her money on a trip to Europe, she owes money to her mother. We called dozens of people without any results. I tried to get to see Marlene Dietrich, but I was thrown out by the doorman.

11 February 1956

All day working on manuscripts for F.C. N.7. [Andrew] Sarris came to help, later Eugene Archer and Arlene Croce. Sarris is working on his review. At midnight we locked him up in our room, so he couldn't escape, and went to 42nd Street to see some movies. We came back at 6 am, Andrew was still working.

18 August 1958

We were shooting the gas station sequence, for Edouard's [de Laurot] film. As Edouard was driving, with Adolfas [Mekas] sitting on the hood, with an Arri, against the traffic, a police car came out of nowhere. They were waiting, hiding. "I am arresting you," said one cop.

They left us on the roadside, and took Edouard to the station. He came back an hour later. "They couldn't understand," said Edouard, "why we were making a film without being paid, just for the love of making it. The cop even called his superior, on the phone, and told him all about our case, asking if such a thing was possible that someone would make a film without being paid."

5 May 1959

Ron Rice called. We met at the Cedar Bar, had a few beers. He says he read my *Voice* column, got all excited, wants to make movies. Did some painting, but decided it wasn't his metier. But now everybody's scaring him about the movie making expenses. Asked what film school he should attend. I said I don't believe in film schools. He agreed. I told him about the 8th Avenue outdated stock place, he said he'll go there. He wanted to start by filming some paintings. I told him it was all wrong, he should leave paintings to the painters. He agreed, and we had a beer to that.

14 July 1960

Every day a dozen envelopes with photographs, credits on the other side, etc., come in, from actors, sending their pictures. So they think we are making a movie about actors? They can't play anything but actors. They look like actors, they speak like actors, they behave like actors, and they are actors. And I hate actors!

Had two weeks of shooting. Today we were scouting for new locations in Conn. Got arrested, all six of us, for trespassing, at a public lake. "I'll slap your asses all over the place," shouted the cop at the police station. He was particularly tough with Adolfas because he thought he was a "beatnik". Adolfas had to grow a beard for his part, so now, wherever we go, we are treated as "beatniks". The cop became mild as a cherry blossom when Barbara [Stone] told him that her brother was the Connecticut State Attorney General. He immediately ordered to let us free, law or no law.

25 July 1960

Sheldon [Rochlin] told me: "I cut my hair for your film. My father told me that my hair was too long. I said, I spent my money on film—the film needs money more than the haircutters do. So he said, cut your hair and I'll buy a share. So I did, without waiting to hear it twice." We now have $500 to continue shooting.

3 August 1960

We set up our cameras by a small lake, in L.I. Just when we were ready to start shooting, a cop came and told us to move. Private Property. He told us, the place belonged to a movie theater chain owner.

Got terribly hungry. No bread, no nothing. Stopped at Almus', in Great Neck, but he himself had nothing. Bought some food in a store and ate it in front of a synagogue, late at night. A rabbi came out to check, so we all fell on our knees, pretending we had come to pray, shouting lines in five different languages, including Latin, which as we later realized, was a wrong way to do it. But we finished our meal in peace. Sheldon went to a nearby house for bread and succeeded in getting some: they thought he was one of the college boys, trying to do something crazy to get into one of the fraternities, or something. They didn't believe he was really hungry.

27 August 1960

Lew Allen and myself, we called another filmmakers' meeting (the Group). Complete confusion. Too many heads. A lot of yapping.

31 August 1960

For the second week now we are living on one meal a day. Once every day we all go to the 77th and Amsterdam corner restaurant to get our one dollar meal. The rest of the day everybody's on his own—to steal, to get from friends, girlfriends, or live on water and air.

Sheldon walks to the icebox every ten minutes, opens it, and closes it again. He knows damn well there is nothing in it. Still, he keeps doing it.

10 September 1960

Last night I spent three hours with Lionel [Rogosin]. He got drunk. Was in one of those moods. Talk, talk, talk, about the New American Cinema. Both got drunk. We were cursing all the businessmen, and S.V., and all the others, and filmmakers who are trying to sell themselves out. We agreed, that most of the filmmakers who are coming to the Group's meetings have hopes that it will be their springboard to Hollywood. After another hour of drunk talk, Lionel said he'll invest in our film $250, I should meet him the next day at six to pick up the check, if he doesn't forget it when he sobers out. He didn't forget it, I got the check. I also got $75 from Amos. Bleibtreu said, he will send $100, a short loan. Things are improving!

16 September 1960

Met Mary Frank on Avenue A. Lent her 50 cents to buy some fruits. Robert is still editing, and out of money. I stood on the corner, overlooking the wet park, waiting for the bus, and cursing the brown trees.

Art, art, art . . . Always goddamn art. Who needs it! And who said, that Kerouac is not literature? Always the same art bull talk. Maya Deren wrote that piece in the *Voice*. Brain creation, intellect, culture, tradition, and all that . . . They are going to teach Robert Frank and Kerouac art! They are going to teach me, who went through the forced labor camps of their culture and their tradition! I put the match to it, pow! Culture and art are O.K. as long as it's not used as a club to hit life on the head.

28 September 1960

Another rambling session of the Group, at Allen's office (165 W. 46th St.). I made a motion that we end the rambling and officially declare that we exist. We voted on it, and my motion was approved by the majority. So now we are the

New American Cinema Group. Later we met at [Emile] de Antonio's place, a few of us. I collected everybody's ideas for the manifesto of the Group which I was entrusted to write. Lionel had to write it with me, but he failed to show up.

30 September 1960

The Group met in the basement of the Bleecker Street Cinema (Lionel owns it and Adolfas is the manager). I presented the first draft of the Group's manifesto, which was approved. Humes suggested to have two manifestoes, and I supported him. He said, he will write one.

A Few Advices to a Beginning Filmmaker:

1. Mistrust every living filmmaker; respect the dead ones.
2. Stay away from the advices of all professional editors. They are all "cutters," literally cutters: they are no editors.
3. Snarl at the criticism and advices of professional cameramen, laugh at "right" or "proper" exposures, focus.
4. Ignore scripts. Shuffle pages around, like Orson did with the script of *Arkadin*.
5. Invent cinema from the beginning, as if nobody had done it before you.

1 October 1960

Robert Frank came, in the morning. We gave him 4000 feet of outdated film for leader. He was tired, angry, beaten down by work, lack of money, businessmen, and contracts. "I'll never make a film like this again," he said. Unshaven, black, tired, he was almost talking to himself.

We lived another day on bread alone. Edouard said, "They say, a man cannot live by bread alone. We can!" De Antonio said: "When they were organizing the American exhibition in Moscow, the State Department screened a 4-hour long version of *Jazz on a Summer Day*, and immediately rejected it. They said, we cannot send to the Russians a film in which blacks and whites are shown together. Besides, they said, the Russians hate jazz."

6 October 1960

No shooting since Monday. Out of money again. Sent Sheldon to Baltimore, to comb his relatives. Borrowed $50 from [Dan] Talbot. Projector broke down, we can't screen our rushes. Adolfas has been fixing it for last two days, machine parts are all over the place—screws, bolts, springs, wheels. To change one small part he had to take the entire machine apart. The repair man wanted to charge us hundreds for the job.

De Antonio called. Said, he found somebody with money. Always, those people with money!

Eugene Archer read the Group's manifesto. He said, it is not for *The New York Times*. It would be good for *The Village Voice,* but not for *The New York Times*. A fool! A manifesto which would suit *The New York Times* wouldn't be a manifesto anymore, it would be a Press Release!

The last meeting of the Group was terribly disappointing. Half of them are ready to lick the *Times*'s feet and Wall Street's floor. So where will they be in a year from now? Humes and Leslie seem to be the only ones who do not give a damn what anybody thinks about them.

1 November 1960

Called Allen. He said, he sunk all his own money into *The Connection*. Those who had promised to invest in it, backed out, politely, waiting for Shirley's "second film": then, they say, they "will invest." They all mistrust, they all want to wait and see. They wait and see how you starve your way through and how you walk the raining night streets beating the walls with your fist—they are waiting to jump after you, if it CLICKS. Let Dante put them into their right place where they can sit and wait, in the eternal fear that they'll lose their goddamn money.

12 December 1960

Now even the weather turned against us. For a month I was planning a screening for today, for possible investors. But yesterday it started snowing. Today New York looks like Alaska, the snow is all over the town. None of the seven investors showed up from their seven hideouts. I spent my last money to pay the projectionist—who came . . . Then we all got into a bus, paying only for three, and went to 87th street, to Diane's place, to see if there is anything in her icebox. There was nothing in it. We collected between all of us 45 cents and sent Sheldon out to buy some bread and tea. He came back with ham and eggs and butter. He managed to steal it all. So we ate and then went to the New Yorker, our last refuge, to see some old Hitchcocks. Dan gave us five bucks to begin life anew. So we walked through the cold, snowy New York streets shouting and singing.

26 December 1960

We interrupted the editing for two days, to celebrate Christmas. Today we all converged into Talbot's office, at the New Yorker, upstairs. De Antonio, Peter (Bogdanovich), Sheldon with Diane, and Dan himself. We drank vodka, ate kelbosa, and made a lot of noise—so much that the projectionist had to come and ask us to be quiet. Peter was imitating Dylan Thomas and Orson Welles; De got completely drunk. We all spilled into the street and continued our party outside.

We tried a new method of editing. We have cards for every shot. We layed them out on a huge reflector. We caught a roach and let it crawl through the cards. But, somehow, the beast chose a very straight line, not interesting at all.

7 January 1961

We had a meeting of the Group at 414 Park Avenue South. Voted to establish our own cooperative distribution center. The only opposition came from Amos [Vogel]. He said, why do we need a new distribution center: Cinema 16 will distribute our films. I pointed out that recently he had rejected several important films, one being Brakhage's *Anticipation of the Night*. Amos said, it's up to him to decide what films can be distributed. He insisted that there is no place for two distribution centers, for the independent film. At which point some became pretty angry. Ron Rice was shouting at Amos, and Amos was shouting at us all. In any case, we have now a center of our own. No film will be rejected from it— that was the first point we all agreed upon. And we are going to run it ourselves.

17 January 1961

Shirley [Clarke], that good woman, she arranged that now, nights, when she is not working, we can use her moviola. She is still working on *The Connection*, shuffling and reshuffling it again. "You know where the key is," she said "so come and work." Just like that. So we brought our footage and worked all night. We'll continue tomorrow night.

20 January 1961

Harrison Starr managed to swing our tapes into Pathe, for a free transfer, so now we are listening and checking our dubbing. We dubbed it right here, in our room, running the film, silently, on moviola, the actors watching their lips, and then immediately after the moviola stops, saying the lines. It worked. Shirley thinks it's a fantastic solution, she'll do the same: no expenses.

Jerome Hill lent us his moviola. Shirley gave 40,000 feet of some used 35mm magnetic tape which we degaussed (through Harrison Starr, for free—he's putting it on some TV program bill)—so now we are in pretty good shape.

16 May 1961

We are in the middle of the moviola tournament fever. Last night Peter [Bogdanovich] came and discovered a new, improved method of turning the frame counter, he almost beat us. The thing is, who will spin more numbers in one turn. Adolfas keeps the record with 137. I come next with 133, which is still a good major league.

Gregory [Markopoulos] was editing his film the last few days at our place. He edited his entire film without a moviola, without even a work print. He is working directly with the negative, original negative. Nothing is going to stop him from completing the film. After the last week's screening, he had to make a few changes. So now he's chopping like a madman. He hates his leading star, he keeps cursing her, and keeps cutting her out wherever he can.

We are switching from beans to oatmeal. Gregory's discovery. He said he made his film (*Serenity*) on oatmeal. Our beans are popping out through our ears and eyes.

29 May 1961

Saturday we locked ourselves up on 43rd Street and with Dan Drasin's and Chuck's help, in one long marathon session, we edited the negative. Hungry and without sleep, but we did it. Chuck fell asleep in the car, on our way to Panna, whom we persuaded to feed us.

Doc (Humes) dropped in, late in the morning, and Bob Kaufman. Walked around the place, slumbering and talking film, until six in the morning. Doc just came back from Cannes, bored with it, telling jokes about Allen Ginsberg and Corso, there, at Cannes, walking around with garbage bags under their arms, in that huge splendorous crowd, searching for a garbage can to dump it out. Then, Nico (Papatakis) telling me how Shirley didn't get the award at Cannes because everybody thought her film (*The Connection*) was a propaganda film for drug addicts.

Doc promised to do something about money, to blackmail somebody. We need $500 this week for *Film Culture*.

20 August 1961

(from a letter to Yoko Ono):
Forgive me for this long silence. I was in the midst of my many duties, there were too many unfinished things concerning Filmmakers' Cooperative and other matters. Now I can tell you something more definitive.

Filmmakers' Cooperative is by now well established and is beginning to do its work. We pushed into the first run theaters four experimental film programs which created a lot of talk in the press and in town. We feel that we are ready by now to invade international waters, and to help our colleagues in other countries. There are two films coming from Italy which we'll help, and the film of Hiroshi, which you discussed in your letter, sounds good and he sould send us a 16mm print (to the Cooperative address).

I am enclosing the first edition of our catalogue—very poor, as you see, but we had to get it out fast. *The Connection* people are waiting for an opening in NY this autumn and they are not willing yet to discuss any foreign sales for another month or so. If anybody is interested to buy the film for Japan, they should write to Shirley Clarke, 372 C.P.W., New York, NY.

No Date 1963

This is our third week in Vermont, shooting *Hallelujah*. Today it's raining. Dark. We open our eyes: raining. We shoot a few scenes, trying to imitate a sunny day. Give up. Shot the lake scenes. Marty doesn't know how to run the motorboat. Circles around like crazy, with the scared actress.

Yesterday we set up the cameras in the middle of a pasture. We needed a shot with some cows. "But where are the cows," I said. "Oh, we can get them here," said the farmer, "they are at the other end of the pasture." The other end! He didn't tell us how wide the goddamn pasture was. David [Stone] and myself had to cross miles of mountainous rocky woods, brooks, got all wet. We crossed woods that neither man nor cow had probably ever crossed. But no goddamn cows! Finally, from the top of a hill, we spotted them: they were a mile or so away, at the other end.

We thought these were domestic animals, cattle, you know. But no. Instead of nice domesticated cows we found wild, scared beasts. At one moment, fifteen of them were running straight at me, in a wild stampede. They chased me back into the woods. Somehow, I don't know how, we succeeded in getting the cows and the actors—twice we lost them all—to the other end of the pasture where the cameras were waiting. And there they stood, angry and wild, camera conscious, staring at us. As soon as we started shooting they stampeded over the camera and ran back into the woods. No force could get them back on that hill. So we gave up. No idea whether we got the footage or not.

Acting: 1958-1965

Taylor Mead

Jerome Hill, Taylor Mead
Hallelujah the Hills

Acting went in many directions in the late 50s and early 60s, including out the window. Happenings often demanded that you not act or assert your personality but behave according to a partly architectural concept of the playwright or non-playwright—stand still, climb a ladder, bounce a ball, jump in a pool, paint yourself blue, take a half-hour to walk across the stage, shout at the audience. Some playwrights counted on the excesses of their actors either personality-wise or drug-induced to evoke myriad connotations from their often simplistic scripts.

Charles Ludlam made his Theatre of the Ridiculous a bizarre and unpredictable event with a strange and unself-conscious group of people delivering lines as if in a dream. On opening night of one of his early plays a board from the proscenium came loose during a scene, whereupon the stage manager brought out a step-ladder downstage center, climbed it, and began hammering the offending board while the cast obliviously went on with the play. In another Ludlam play, *Big Hotel,* Jack Smith, playing a bellhop, is ordered to register a Santa Claus who has dropped dead in the lobby and take him to his room (upstairs). Taking his time as usual, Jack Smith spends some 20 minutes or more doing same, to the uproar of the audience. It was more than acting—it was a deadly serious game of life for Jack and Charles and a host of others. Even though some of the plays written later seem quite bizarre, the content from the acting point of view seems a bit more predictable and less "dangerous."

In the field of acting I received some training at the Pasadena Playhouse, but after nine months of a rather rigid course including history of costumes, fencing, history of theatre, and not enough acting, and too much homework (reminiscent of boarding school), I began to rebel against all of the traditional private over-schooling. About this time, in the 40s, I picked up on George Bernard Shaw and for the next several years did almost nothing but read Shaw. I returned to my home in Detroit for awhile and then began hitchhiking all over the United States; returned again to work for Merrill Lynch as a broker-in-training but after reading Jack Kerouac's *On The Road* and Allen Ginsberg's *Howl* was off again. Went to San Francisco in the mid-50s (hitchhiking) at the height of the Beat movement—savored excitement in air but was frightened out of North Beach area by an over-zealous police sergeant and his unconstitutional Black Maria. Went to New York and studied for a year with Herbert Berghof (one of the founders of Actors Studio—his exhortation to actors was to be able to go from their street selves into their "acting" scenes with a minimum of connivance and contrivance and to avoid "thought" or "thinking" on stage).

Took off on the road again and wound up in L.A. and San Francisco. I introduced myself to the now waning Beat movement in San Francisco by reading poetry in cafés. There was beginning to be a general resistance to outsiders but some of my more scatological and defiant poems overcame the often rowdy jaded bar and coffeehouse crowds. They thought they'd seen it all. I met Jack Kerouac and we had instant rapport. Nancy Mitford and Kenneth Tynan were visiting from England and at a poetry contest they awarded the permanent resident poet Bob Kaufman and myself 1st prize—I forget what it was. Through my readings I came to know Ron Rice—recently arrived from New York and a brief stint at the Cooper Union film school. He conceived the idea to photograph me with a borrowed 16mm movie camera wandering among the denizens and architecture of San Francisco, relating to what few "beat" people had stayed on or survived. With Ron, between the idea and the doing there was very little pause. By hook or by crook he was determined to film. His girlfriend helped us out, often very unwillingly, and we churned out *The Flower Thief*. It was received very well at the coffeehouses, but Ron was discouraged that the "big boys" from Hollywood weren't knocking on his door. At one point he announced a public burning of the film— at another he wanted to pour a blue wash over it and cut it into abstract mixed up segments. I fought this move vehemently and told him this was probably the last of the Beat scene in S.F. and it was at the least a splendid documentary. The acting was definitely no-frills—we all just had a good time and with Ron behind the camera there was definitely no self-consciousness on anyone's part.

I think, besides the general "beat" feeling and the influence of the anti-"striving for success" atmosphere, we were encouraged by the film *Pull My Daisy* which came out around this time. This was a fascinating film about spontaneous people, far from thoughts of "Plot." But even *Pull My Daisy* was big business as far as Ron and I were concerned. It must have cost many thousands and we barely had hundreds. Ron used out of date World War II machine-gun film which fortunately had a wonderful soft quality photographically and was very cheap. All our actors were free or cost a few jugs of wine and some "grass," which they often brought themselves. We knew our daily lifestyle was enough, so we didn't bother to "act." Sometimes we made a few expansive gestures and a little extra drama in deference to the Hollywood idea and the fun of pretending we might be stars! When *The Flower Thief* showed a summer later in New York at a lower east side movie house it just happened the critics had nothing much to do that season and we were written up in all the papers of New York and many national magazines.

When the films appeared first in San Francisco without any but local North Beach publicity several young filmmakers asked me to improvise for their cameras. One fellow was Vernon Zimmerman, and we decided to use the old mansions in another section of San Francisco (many were empty and soon to be demolished). For this film, *Lemon Hearts*, I imagined people who might have inhabited the houses and created about eight different roles—a cardinal or pope blessing people from the bay window of an old mansion (intercut with stock crowd shots) and finally spitting on them, "giving up" on them and throwing his palm fronds at them in disgust. I also played both a young swain proposing to a shy over-demure girlfriend, and the girlfriend; also an eccentric superintendant, etc. . . . or, as the L.A. Times recently said, I was the

"quintessential outsider." My acting of course had a lot to do with the books I read and the mood of the times—the prevailing attitudes of the disenfranchised and the fun of being able to say and do almost anything—the more ironic and "strange" the better. We really felt and knew we were pushing the freedoms of the United States in order to give them a little exercise. A year or two later *Lemon Hearts* was awarded the Rosenthal Award at The Museum of Modern Art in New York as the best film by a young director—I believe Vernon Zimmerman was 25.

After six months in San Francisco I moved to Venice, a beach community on the edge of L.A. In spite of the great friends in S.F., I found the city depressing with its nightly chilling fog and not enough money to at least spend the evening in one of its many cozy expensive restaurants. Also there was a heavy alcohol scene now among the Beats and their buddies—and many of the poets had disappeared for one reason or another—some beginning to earn enough from their books to travel in more style.

There was an interesting and warmer scene going on in Venice with several exciting coffee houses and a beautiful old building called The Gas House run by Eric Nord from San Francisco who was hospitable to everyone and allowed us free reign at our poetry, theater, and Happenings evenings. I slept on the beach or in the back stairwell of The Gas House or on the floor of the Venice West Coffee House. I soon became involved in another fun film project—very few of the hundred or more films I've been involved in could be described as "work"—and nobody got up before noon. In fact several years and many films later while watching TV with Andy Warhol during the filming of *San Diego Surf* in La Jolla, California, we heard Barbara Stanwyck describe how she got up at 5 or 6 every morning to be on the set and do "take" after "take" for the rest of the day—Andy turned to the rest of us and said, "Instead of starting to shoot at noon tomorrow let's wait until three."

The film I became involved with in Venice, circa 1961, was called *Passion In A Seaside Slum,* directed by Bob Chatterton, a movie buff, who bought an 8mm camera and said, "O.K. Taylor, let's go." I played eight or more roles in this film—all bizarre, outrageous, non-pornographic but upsetting to many mores. In the last scene I descend a winding staircase on a huge oil storage tank in a rockettes costume and go off into the sunset with a policeman. Everything about the film was illegal at the time, including our use of private property. Our audiences found it hilarious. However, one person I admired enormously was shocked—Stan Laurel. Bob Chatterton was a very close friend of Laurel's, so we took the film to his apartment in Santa Monica to show him and his wife. Mrs. Laurel loved it, but Stan was shocked. Sometime later though, he admitted to being amused.

After Venice, I spent many months in Mexico purchasing my own 16mm camera at the National Pawn Shop in Mexico City, and photographing my travels, often one frame at a time, and then showing it as a movie. I was awarded a New York State Council of the Arts grant on the basis of these personal "Home Movies." I was helped to relax even more in front of the camera by the experience of being behind it.

Back in New York, I literally fell into various movie and theater projects. I was much too shy to "make the rounds"—I never "paid my dues" as the pros love to say. I think many of the people who "make it" are more aggressive and insensitive and "push" somehow wins out over talent. I have seen so many splendid actors, not only in everyday life but in acting schools, who either were ignored by the powers that be or who couldn't take the rejections and scorching eyes of would-be employers, not to mention the limited quality-work available. In many ways, though, I wish I had been a little more thick-skinned and pushed my way into the money field.

From among the people who were familiar with my poetry and films, several wonderful offers, quality-wise, came my way—no audition required: *Hallelujah The Hills* by Adolfas Mekas, *Open The Door And See All The People* by Jerome Hill, *Babo 73* by Robert Downey, *The Queen of Sheba Meets The Atom Man* by Ron Rice—and then a long series of films with Andy Warhol, one of the easiest, least intimidating people to work for (difficult in other areas). In 1963, we drove to California for an opening of his paintings—at the time he was afraid to fly. He had recently purchased a movie camera and made the film *Sleep* in New York. This time he decided to add a little plot and some complications and I was a logical Tarzan, being opposite to the type. In Hollywood we enlisted Dennis Hopper, John Houseman, Claes and Patty Oldenburg, and other natives, and made ourselves a very "laid back" jungle film. [*Tarzan and Jane Regained—Sort Of.*] It was unscripted as were most of the films and the directions involved "look tough" or "swim across the Beverly Hills Hotel pool."

Andy didn't like too much "acting." In fact Kim Novak is one of his favorite stars. When we were filming *Lonesome Cowboys,* five years later in Arizona, I became over-enthusiastic about what was supposed to be happening—he simply said, "too much plot" and I cooled it. He wanted more of a personal, real interchange among the "actors" rather than a "story."

I have had occasion to use my training as an actor frequently. In 1964, Jerry Benjamin cast me in a Frank O'Hara play, *The General Returns From One Place To Another,* in which I played a sort of General MacArthur, in tandem with a play by Amiri Baraka (LeRoi Jones), *The Baptism,* in which I played a preacher. I had to fall back on all the disciplines of school and "method" for the rather harsh demands of the script and director. Not a pleasant rehearsal experience compared to the relative ball with my anarchist film directors. However, I managed to be awarded an Obie for my part as the general and Frank O'Hara dedicated the play "to Warner Brothers and Taylor Mead."

Shirley Clarke: An Interview

Melinda Ward

Melinda Ward

Shirley Clarke

Shirley Clarke began her artistic career as a modern dancer. In the early 1950s she turned from dancing to making dance films with choreographers Daniel Nagrin and Anna Sokolow. Clarke developed a camera and editing style which could be called choreographic even when applied to such non-dance subject matter as bridges and skyscrapers which she did in 1958–59. *The Connection,* made in 1960, is a landmark in American independent feature filmmaking because of its realistic presentation of a marginal lifestyle (junkies in a loft waiting for their "connection"), its critical success and its censorship battles. The making of *The Connection* and Clarke's other two 60s features included in this retrospective, *The Cool World* and *Portrait of Jason,* put her at the center of the first struggles to create an American independent feature film movement. We asked her to give us her version of this history.

This is how I remember our history. In the 50s, Morris Engel made *The Little Fugitive.* Lionel Rogosin had done *On The Bowery.* By the end of the 50s, a number of us wanted to make features. And so we met up at Lew Allen's office—Robert Frank, Jonas [Mekas], [Emile] de Antonio and a lot of the New York filmmakers—about 10 altogether. What we decided to do was to form a kind of "co-op" and together raise money to produce and distribute 10 films. The idea was that for one investment of say $1,000, the backer would end up owning a piece of each of the 10 films. The next idea was to find investors who though they might not trust one of us separately, with a piece of each of us, they would figure they couldn't lose. We were reinventing the Hollywood Studio—without realizing it. What we really needed was a Louis B. Mayer. What we got were a lot of filmmakers that couldn't agree about anything together. I guess we all wanted to go it alone—*independent* filmmakers. Even my producer and the backers of *The Connection* wanted a more experienced distributor for "their" film and not a new and untried organization. But Jonas went ahead with the idea of a "cooperative" of filmmakers, I tried to help and the Filmmakers' Cooperative got started. The filmmakers who were interested in the Co-op turned out to be those who were mostly making short experimental films like Brakhage and Ed Emshwiller. The rest of us, on our own, started to find separate ways of raising money, many different ways (though for years the Co-op distributed some of my short films). The kind of financing that many of us used was to sell shares of the film—this worked because the tax law said that if an investor lost money he could take it off his taxes. And there were a lot of "rich art-lover" types around who found it fun to be involved in what they considered new exciting filmmaking. We based our thinking on the Broadway theater and how it was financed. Lewis Allen, who ended up producing *The Connection* for me, was actually a Broadway producer. Our model was the Broadway theater—backers owned shares in the production.

Then in the mid-60s, some of us came back together again, Lionel, myself, Jonas and Adolfas Mekas. I think Adolfas at that point was finally producing his films and the Co-op had been doing very well for the experimental films and we felt we should try something for the feature filmmakers, for the independent features, and the "underground" films. So we started something called Filmmakers Distribution Center to distribute our features in commercial situations. We hired Louis Brigante to head it up and we actually had some financial and critical successes. The biggest success I guess had to be Warhol's *Chelsea Girls*. We even made some money from our films. I mean no individual film made a great deal of money but we managed to exist and make a number of very good films for about three years. The problem was we never had enough capital to open and properly publicize the films or to find enough independent theater owners like Max Laemmle in California, Louis Sher in the Midwest and Rugoff on the East Coast (though a lot of my films did very well in Europe). Part of what happened was that eventually Andy Warhol or the people around him said to him, "Look you don't need that organization. They're just living off you. You can do better on your own," and he proceeded to drop out. It was never unfriendly, it was just realistic. The Filmmakers Distribution Center did distribute *Portrait of Jason* for me with some success. Probably nowhere near the success it would have had had it been a commercial organization, but we had a lot to learn about commercial distribution and I for one surely needed the Distribution Center. After all, how many people would have taken *Jason* at that time? Dan Talbot when he formed New Yorker Films a year later took *Jason*. But it was the Distribution Center that opened the film in their little theater (run by the Co-op in the basement of a building on 41st Street) and as a result of that run the film got invited to play at the New York Film Festival at Lincoln Center. It was after the Lincoln Center success that Dan took it over.

How did you go about making your first feature?

By 1959–60, I was convinced that I really wanted to do a feature. My short films didn't seem to give me enough space. My sister, Elaine Dundy, who was married to theater critic Kenneth Tynan, suggested that I make a film based on the play, *The Connection*. I thought it was a great idea because I loved the play—it fascinated me. I got friendly with its author, Jack Gelber, and he agreed that I could option the play and together we'd do a film script. Then, I'd try to raise the money and direct the film. It was at this point that I met Lewis Allen, again through my sister. She knew that Lew had a film company and that he wanted to make films but as yet had never made one. He was interested and told me he would let me know in a few days if he could raise the money with the help of a stock broker who was his partner. His plan was to raise the money from his theater sources and the broker's clients. Basically he was raising money as if he was going to do a Broadway show, which was what he had been doing for years. Two days later he called me and said okay and so we went ahead and made *The Connection*. Through the good auspices of Gene Moskowitz who was on *Variety* in Paris, the film was chosen to go to the Cannes Film Festival and I went with it. That was a great coup!

Was there a better reception in Europe than in America?

Oh my god! It was absolutely fabulous. It was just extraordinary what happened at Cannes. We were the absolute hit of that festival. There was not a girl in a pink bikini with a pink poodle and pink hair that got photographed that year in Cannes. All the "Beat" Americans in Europe came to Cannes to support us, in their Volkswagon buses and cars—they slept on the beach—god knows how they managed—but their "look" was the hit of the festival that May and they got photographed all the time. They enchanted the European press. Also, Allen Ginsberg, Gregory Corso and Peter Orlovsky, some of the actors and jazz musicians from the film came with me (they had been doing the play in London). The festival gave us a villa to live in and we just took over the whole place. Allen became our nice Jewish uncle who made sure we got fed. The festival people had given us a place to sleep, but they hadn't given us very much money to eat with so we really did a lot of very interesting hustling and met a lot of people. The European press went wild for this new American scene—"Les Beatniks" right? And it ended up with the head of the festival at Cannes, M. Fauve-Lebret, giving a dinner party for me. All the critics were invited to come to dinner and meet me and he said, "Any film you ever do, Madame, from now on is invited to play at Cannes." I mean I was insane. I was out of my mind. I couldn't figure out what was happening at all. And then we came back to the United States of America and guess what? Censorship!

How real was the censorship?

It was two years real, it stopped the film from opening in New York City and perhaps it destroyed the film's success—no, that's not totally true but certainly it partially destroyed the potential success of *The Connection* in the United States. If it had been able to open here right after Cannes, with all the publicity that had filtered back to the United States at the time, it would have been wonderful. But the film was censored in New York City and we had to go to court for two years before it could open. Ephraim London, who had just won the case against religious censorship for the film, *The Miracle* with Anna Magnani was looking for a film to challenge the censorship law on obscenity. The "obscenity" that they challenged in *The Connection* was, you won't believe it, the word "shit" and it was used by the junkies mostly to describe the drug, heroin. The word expressed their self-contempt. The other thing censored was a shot of one of the actors going through a male nudie magazine. I had used a little, quick shot of it in the film because I thought it was cute, a normal thing for one of the bored junkies to do. And that's why we went to court. It was a very, very long and trying experience. First of all because it cost a good deal of money, second because the courts kept stalling and refusing to hear the case. As a result of the success of the screening in Cannes, Irving Shapiro, a well known distributor of foreign films, agreed to be our distributor. But because of not being able to get a license he couldn't open the film and he was losing money . . . I kept saying, "We've got to do something drastic. Maybe we've got to show the film somehow and maybe even get arrested or something because soon nobody but us is going to care whether they ever see it." Then finally Irving got hold of a newly renovated theater in the Broadway area and they agreed to take a chance and open the film. We invited Bosley Crowther to come to the opening at 10 in the morning so that he could watch me and the projectionist get arrested for showing the movie. He wrote a good Sunday column on censorship, though not necessarily a great review of the film. But the plan worked, Ephraim London could then move in. And the case was finally heard by the court and we won! Somehow it was a great victory that we could now say "shit" in the movies. Though this case finally broke the back of censorship, alas, for us it still took another six months of going through the courts. Somehow along the way the potential audience got lost somewhere.

Shirley Clarke directing *The Connection*

There's quite a stylistic difference between *The Connection* and your second feature, *The Cool World*. The latter is less "theatrical" and more "documentary" in style. So many of the films of this period combine documentary and fictional elements.

But that's also true of *The Connection*. I used, on purpose, a documentary style in the shooting and in the acting to create a greater sense of reality. All the camera movements were basically improvised by me as we went along (we shot in sequence) to create the kind of "spontaneity" inherent in the documentary. The actors were encouraged to improvise "on camera."

The next thing that happened was important to the direction I was to take in my feature films. In order to raise money, Lew Allen would bring potential backers (we still needed them) to the editing room to watch me edit on Sundays. One of the people he brought was Fred Wiseman. Fred was a criminal lawyer and he liked what he saw and put up $3,000 or something. Now, Fred really wanted to make movies himself and he thought that a very good way to learn might be to produce a movie for someone whose work he liked. And so that's how we got together. After *The Connection* finally opened he took me to see Warren Miller who had worked with Robert Rossen turning his novel of *The Cool World* into a Broadway play. The play failed after two performances and Warren and Bob Rossen were so distressed and turned off by the experience that they wanted nothing more to do with it. The rights reverted to Warren and he said to Fred and me, "Okay, I know you and I know your work and whatever you want to do it's okay with me. Just leave me out." Fred Wiseman also trusted me. Everyone's faith in me was fabulous and it still means a lot to me. Then I wrote the script from the novel. I had decided to do a script on my own without reading the play. A friend of mine, the black actor, Carl Lee (he'd been in *The Connection*), helped me. Carl and I and a Polaroid camera drove around Harlem a lot and got to know streets that were to make up the life and texture of the film. I was able to write scenes for the locations that I knew we'd actually be able to use.

My thinking about reality in films started a long time back in a very funny way. I had been a member of Cinema 16 which had shown my experimental films for years. I went on a safari with them to Eastman House in the mid-50s. We were shown a film [*They Won't Forget*] about a lynching with Lana Turner in it. I found it very false. I did not believe it at all. I *totally* didn't believe it. To my eye and the way I saw things, all that klieg lighting so carefully lighting Lana Turner (a so properly coiffeured and neatly dressed Lana) who was supposed to be witnessing a lynching in a square in the South somewhere was just *not* believable. And I said to myself, "That's not the way I would make a film. That just looks silly." By *The Cool World*, I already knew something about shooting in the streets because by then I'd been on the streets doing the *Brussels Loop* for Willard Van Dyke—little three-minute films for the Brussels World Fair that I made with Donn Pennebaker. Penny had traveled around the country and I had traveled around the streets of New York. I shot films about people and their body language with each other, as a way of showing the kind of "melting pot" look that makes up America. After *The Loops* I got the chance to make a film about the construction of a building called *Skyscraper*. That film also took place in the streets of New York.

There's a significant difference between the very formalistic, beautifully composed urban documentary imagery of the 1930s and the less-polished look after World War II. It has to do with the available camera technology, doesn't it?

You're absolutely right. The development of the professional hand-held cameras changed not only styles but allowed for new concepts. *The Cool World* was shot entirely with a hand-held 35mm camera. We had a blimp specially built for the camera with the ability to handle a zoom lens specially motorized by Mitch Bogdonevitch (a great mechanical genius). The technical people around us developed many improvements that are still used to this day. Also, the Nagra tape recorder (portable and with very high quality sound) had been invented by then, which allowed us to make hand-held features. As a matter of fact the one we used in *The Cool World* was one of the last Nagras that Kudulski made himself. And I still have it! Yes, technology is always changing art.

You talked about working with Pennebaker. Could you discuss your attitudes toward documentary and cinema verité.

Actually my argument is not so much with Pennebaker as it is with Ricky Leacock, though Ricky often vacillates, as do I. We're never faithful to our causes! The basic argument went like this: I would say to Ricky, "Okay now for instance, I'm walking down a city street and I see a drunk lying in the gutter and, as I'm watching, two little boys see the drunk. Then they see a policeman coming down the street so they rush up to the drunk and drag him away before the cop can arrest him. Now unfortunately, that day I didn't happen to have a camera with me. Yet it's a wonderful scene and I want to put it in a movie, so what I do is 'recreate' it for my film." But Ricky says, "Nope. That's theatrical filmmaking not real." The answer of course is not "nope." I believe that a documentary and dramatic mix makes for better, more believable films, like the Italian neo-realists. Actually at the time that I was doing *The Cool World,* Penny and Ricky were doing that film of theirs about a Puerto Rican gang in East Harlem. The problem they had was that their leading guy got sent to jail so there were all sorts of things that had to get narrated because they couldn't control "real" life.

For me there is another important difference and that is, if you want to have very tender, quiet, intimate moments, you really need actors, you need performers who are able to express what you need when the camera is rolling. Of course, they can be "real" people like the children in *The Cool World* but they have to be able to act believably on cue. There is a very fine line here. I guess it becomes a personal aesthetic judgment. I have been vacillating all my life between wanting to be a great ballerina, on one hand, and the leader of a revolution on the other—meaning that I'm endlessly trying to be both realistic and abstract at the same time. So sometimes I do something realistic like *The Cool World*. But the camera in that film is just as choreographed as it was for *The Connection* or *Portrait of Jason* or even one of my dance films. That's what "cinematic" means to me.

How do you perceive the difference between the mid-60s and today in all the things that we've talked about such as censorship, funding, distribution? Have things like the National Endowment for the Arts made a difference in the kind of film that you're interested in doing?

Well, I finally did get a grant to finish *Tongues* from the N.E.A. but I never before got a grant from them. I've never gotten a Guggenheim or a lot of grants at all. I did get very important support from the New York State Council on the Arts, which made it possible for me to have access to the technology to explore video. The grant world can start you off but it cannot give you the rest of your artistic life. And, in the art forms like film or video, they really can't give enough money to make a feature film or a major "state of the art" video feature. Actually what I see as a more hopeful way to make feature films or video are organizations like Independent Feature Project.

I've watched them over the years and their organization seems to be getting stronger and better and more successful all the time. The independent filmmakers of the 70s—Richard Pierce, Bob Young, etc., have somehow been able to continue making films *they* want to make *independently*. They seem to be finding some way to get the necessary money and yet maintain personal control. There are still many different ways of raising money. I guess in a way that has always been true in American filmmaking and, hopefully, always will be. I suspect that there are going to be a lot more independent low-budget films in the future partly due to the new technologies and partly because Hollywood has gotten so totally insane with the $40 million flicks. In my opinion the greatest value of independent filmmaking has always been its innovation. Strangely enough, *not* having billions of dollars often helps the creative process—the problem-solving part. For instance in that new film, *Chan Is Missing,* you can see that a lack of money led to a fresh, new, creative style. That's how the art of filmmaking develops.

Working with a low budget can be very frustrating though. Even after you finally manage to make the film, you often have to spend years distributing it yourself.

You know even when they make Hollywood movies, most of the time it takes three years. For all of us, the wonderful period is while the film is being made, but after that there's the distribution, the reviews, etc. Watching what happens then can be tough. I don't know why anybody should feel any more sorry for the lot of the low-budget independent filmmaker than the precarious life of the studio filmmaker nowadays. It's hard work for anyone to make any film. The independent filmmakers we are talking about are really not commercial enough for a mass audience. We don't seem to have, yet, a large enough audience for a wonderful little film like *Chan is Missing*. Successful as it is, it's not going to be a blockbuster. Fortunes will not be made on it. They weren't on *Shadows*, they weren't on *The Connection*, they weren't on *The Cool World*, etc., etc.

Actually, the only movie I ever really made money on and still make money on is *Portrait of Jason* and that is because it didn't cost much. It cost $25,000, the whole damn thing, and it only cost that much because there was a scratch across the entire negative that had to be removed. That cost $5,000, then another $5,000 went into the distribution. But after New Yorker Films distributed it, I started to make a little money.

What about the support networks—schools now teaching filmmakers, media arts centers, the National Endowment for the Arts, other foundations that support the independent film? Haven't they made a difference?

I will tell you something I find interesting, though I guess not surprising. After I'd been at UCLA for about four years, they finally showed my films in their big theater. That's how much real support even your own university gives. You know, there is only one course given each year on avant-garde and independent films at UCLA. Otherwise the students study Hollywood movies, a few foreign films, and the old classics. Also, it is harder and harder for new filmmakers coming in. Now that there are so many of them, it's not getting easier. I suspect it was much easier for me when I started than it is for young people starting now. Like I said there were only a few of me.

What has surprised us in working on this retrospective, is discovering how many people have not seen the films. You are right. They aren't taught. They aren't seen.

You know Cocteau's films were not widely known when they first came out and they have gotten widely known because of what people like yourself did and what you're doing now. For instance I don't know how many young people know René Clair's work any longer. To me that's incredible because his films are not only wonderful on their own but they greatly influenced Chaplin, Fellini and many others. Me too. A great deal of my personal filmmaking is based on the concepts and styles that René Clair introduced to the movies—realistic scenes mixed with naturalistic dancing and singing in the streets. One of the things I hope to do is to acknowledge my indebtedness to him in my electronic musical comedy video feature that I'm in the process of making. I plan to dedicate it to René Clair. I love his movies but they get harder and harder to see anywhere.

Distribution really does have everything to do with the evolution of style. It's only when films are available that they are able to have an influence. For instance, weren't Italian neo-realist films seen by you and other young filmmakers after World War II?

Oh god, yes. Rossellini! That's the other filmmaker who really got to me. When I saw Rossellini's films I knew I could make the kind of movie I wanted to make. When Joseph Burstyn and Arthur Mayer first brought those films to America, they could only play them in a crumby little theater in New York called the World Theater (it had the best fleas in town). I saw all the Italian neo-realist films there and I was bowled over by the fact that they looked so really "real." I was very excited—something clicked for me. I understood something important that was going to change my way of filmmaking. (Up to then I'd been making dance films.) I expect the same thing happened to a lot of filmmakers and a lot of audiences. Also it is important to note that Burstyn and Mayer wrote about the films and worked hard to get those films popular in America. They helped to change film history.

Film is also influenced at different times by the other arts.

Have you ever tried to figure out which came first? We know that Abstract Expressionism, Be-Bop music and experimental filmmaking were all happening at the same time. We were all reacting to the social realities of our time in much the same way. Just like now when there is a punk movement in all the arts. It is an enormous battle against the terror of annihilation. That's what artists do, express their personal reactions to their world, and when a lot of them do it, it becomes a movement.

Do you find that in some of today's independent feature films and documentaries there's a tendency to look at historical periods of time rather than responding to the present?

Yes, sometimes there are periods when that happens. Art seems to alternate between the reactionary look backward and the radical leap forward. That's just the way it goes. Then at a certain point something really takes off, really clicks, (I think—I *hope* we're about to have that click). At the point we decide not to die, not to let the holocaust take over, our art will reflect it. Art is always a part of humanity's survival, often even a part of the solution for that survival. Somehow, at times of crisis in human history, there often seems to be a renaissance in the arts. The artists are very often the clarion callers, "Yes, yes, we *can* go on." I remember the 50s, the McCarthy era, as such a terrible time. I thought that some of my radical artist friends, myself included, were going to be killed or sent to prison. You know? We thought we were going to be done in; fascism was going to take over. Somehow, it didn't. Not quite. And now, all of us with any sense at all know that for this planet to survive into the 21st century—boy, it's going to take a lot from all of us.

The Savage Eye
Shadows

Jonathan Rosenbaum

Ben Carruthers *Shadows*

"I don't think that anything related to *Shadows* was documentary," John Cassavetes remarked in an interview published in *Films and Filming* (February 1961). Yet it seems impossible to discuss the film's meaning and impact without some reference to the documentary tradition. Just as *The Savage Eye* situates its own fictional and dramatic narrative within and against a specific documentary sense of place—a Los Angeles perceived through the lenses of Jack Couffer, Helen Levitt, Haskell Wexler (feature photographers), Sy Wexler and Joel Coleman (contributing photographers)—*Shadows* depends no less crucially on a Manhattan (mainly midtown) perceived by the touristic setups of cameraman Erich Kollmar and his assistant Al Ruban. Significantly, the natural locations and background milieu in both films structure the dramatic shape of many scenes, as if they themselves were producing the narratives.

At the beginning of *Shadows,* for instance, the three central characters—a young and alienated mulatto hipster (Ben Carruthers), his black older brother who sings in nightclubs (Hugh Hurd), and their 20-year-old, light-skinned flirtatious sister (Lelia Goldoni)—are introduced in separate improvised scenes, and each of these is framed by a specific location and milieu that the camera presents as a documentary subject. The extraordinary ambiance of the actors' sensitivities is conveyed at once throughout this beginning, which glitters with sudden observations that register like personal discoveries.

Behind the credits, Ben is seen at a crowded, noisy party where loud rock music is playing, completely isolated from the surrounding activity—working his way around the room's edges with arms upraised, lurking in one corner like James Dean in a trapped animal pose, essentially trying to remain alone in the midst of a mob. In every technical aspect, from the grainy texture of the image to the eliptical and fragmentary nature of the editing, a documentary manner is directly evoked, and in such a way that the narrative fiction, Ben* in his isolation, seems almost stumbled upon—one followed thread in a tangle of apparently limitless actuality.

** The actors' use of their own full names in* Shadows*—curtailed only by the avoidance of surnames for Benny and Lelia further extends the illusion that all three are blood relatives (when in fact none are, and Goldoni is entirely white)—naturally carries the documentary aesthetic further, and invests their improvisation with existential significance, an acting and playing out of their own identities. By contrast, the actors in* The Savage Eye *take on wholly assumed identities.*

After a second sequence introducing Hugh at a rehearsal, the scene shifts to Hugh and Lelia at Port Authority Bus Terminal as he's about to leave for a singing gig in Philadelphia. The gentle tension at work between siblings here is about whether she should take a cab home, a suggestion she rejects because she insists she's old enough to take care of herself. After Hugh leaves, Lelia pauses to look at posters of Brigitte Bardot outside a Times Square theater until a man sidles up to her and grabs her arm (as if to bear out the wisdom of Hugh's paternalistic warning about her walking home alone). Another man—recognizable as Cassavetes in a brief cameo—gruffly pushes the masher away, allowing Lelia to break loose and hurry off, and the shot ends after she has fled, with the camera focused ominously on the nearby Rialto marquee, which reads: *Models by Day Playgirls by Night Girls Inc.*
She Stops at Nothing to Get What She Wants
also *Impulse*
—a conclusion that uses documentary to amplify the fiction.

This leads us logically enough to the opening of *The Savage Eye,* and a contrasting set of strategies in juxtaposing documentary and fiction. Here we begin with no characters or milieux in the ordinary sense, merely a plane arriving in the Los Angeles airport and glimpses of emerging passengers. Then two actorly presences take over and guide our attention in two separate and distinct directions—towards an abstract perception of the passengers in general, bolstered by the documentary look and context and by a disembodied male, quasi-authorial voice (that of Gary Merrill), and a concrete perception of one passenger in particular (the fictional Judith McGuire), played by actress Barbara Baxley, who crosses the airport and boards a bus. As the camera again seems to pick out one isolated thread from a tangle of actuality (a standard neo-realist approach), these two visual registers, documentary and fiction, become complemented by the two voices on the soundtrack, establishing a dialogue between these modes that, in contrast to *Shadows,* reduces the behavioral density of characters and increases their sociological context and background through an offscreen literary text:

Merrill: Travellers by cloud—uneasy, grateful, swung on a thread of exploding fire, they step down from heaven to the great sweaty footbound company of us all—Alone, traveller?
Baxley: Alone.
Merrill: What's your name?
Baxley: Judith.
Merrill: Judith what?
Baxley: Judith X.
Merrill: What's the X?
Baxley: Ex-McGuire.[. . .]
Merrill: Alone, traveller?
Baxley: Alone.
Merrill: Why?
Baxley: Because the touch of human skin makes me sick.
Merrill: What's his name?
Baxley: Who?
Merrill: You ex-husband.
Baxley: Charles McGuire.
Merrill: How long did it last?
Baxley: Nine years, sixty-four days.
Merrill: Children?
Baxley: Killed.
Merrill: Killed? How?
Baxley: The usual way. Rubber, miscarriage, misconception, the knife. . . . Who are you?
Merrill: I'm your angel. Your double. That wild dreamer—your conscience. Your god. Your ghost. . . . Where are we going?
Baxley: I don't much care.
Merrill: To the past—or the future? To the seven layers of Troy? To London burning by war? Or Rome with the searchers of the catacombs? Or Athens, Los Angeles? Cities of the moon?
Baxley: Well, hardly. I only paid $1.25.

It's a strained literary mode which seems to reflect the preoccupations and poetics of lapsed Catholicism, the voices bouncing back and forth at times like the queries and responses in a catechism. Significantly, the characters in this dialogue—Judith and The Poet (as Merrill is identified in the credits)—also suggest at times the disembodied voices in a tortured version of a confessional: the woman almost constantly visible, and acutely vulnerable in her visibility; the father-confessor-god-poet speaking safely and snugly from half-outside the fiction—apparently seeing all, knowing all and risking nothing.

Sounding at times like T.S. Eliot strained through pulp—and abetted by a remarkable performance from Baxley and a Leonard Rosenmann score whose abrasive atonality equally summons up a veritable anthology of purple prose-poetry read to mannerist 50s music (from Ken Nordine's *Word Jazz* to June Christy and Stan Kenton's *This is My Theme* to the collaborations of poets like Kerouac and Rexroth with jazz musicians)—the commentary throughout *The Savage Eye* extends and clarifies the studied anti-humanism of the visuals, which, in keeping with the film's title, tends to rely on the grotesque images of satire: a garishly opulent rotating cowgirl figure in front of a motel, a nosejob operation which is virtually contemporaneous with the one performed in Thomas Pynchon's *V,* a little girl with false eyelashes in a hat store, a dog's funeral. According to Joseph Strick (in an interview with Judith Christ in the *New York Herald-Tribune,* June 5, 1960), "Our first idea was Los Angeles as seen by Hogarth. The appurtenances

have changed, but life is not so very different. Then we realized the parallel was too stretched for a film."

Although *The Savage Eye* is co-signed equally by Strick, Ben Maddow and Sidney Meyers, it appears from the same interview that Maddow was principally responsible for the script. The literary bent of Strick, however, should not be overlooked; at the time of the film's New York release, he cited *Ulysses* and *The Castle* among his future film projects with Maddow and Meyers, and regarding *The Savage Eye,* noted, "We're hoping Sartre, Cocteau or Malraux will contribute the French script. In Italy, we hope to get Carlo Levi or Ignazio Silone to do the soundtrack. In the Spanish version—it's the kind of thing you'd like Lorca to do if he were alive."

The visible humanism of Meyers (as evidenced by *The Quiet One,* his previous film) and Helen Levitt, among other collaborators, seems a bit harder to reconcile with the film's misanthropy—although the latter recently recalled, in a brief phone conversation with the author, that little of her own work was used in the final version. (She mainly recollects going around with Strick and filming "everything that appealed to us," including "a lot of oil pumps and places in Venice" and the dinosaurs in the La Brea Tar Pits.) For Jonas Mekas, the film's heartlessness could be accounted for geographically, like a documentary fact rather than like a state of mind:

. . . Perhaps the shadow-killing and all-leveling California sun affects one differently (which may also be the reason for what Hollywood really is)—basically, the West Coast filmmakers seem to take life as a plain, one-level phenomenon, without any shadows or nooks or corners. In this shadow-less sun all the proportions of life seem to have been bleached out. Death, Birth, Sickness, Sex—everything acquires the color of a wax museum. Even Sidney Meyers' The Savage Eye, *as it is, with its cynical detachment, can be explained only by the fact that it was shot in California. In New York the same scenes would have acquired a certain sadness, a certain humaneness. ("Cinema of the New Generation,"* Film Culture *No. 21, Summer 1960)*

One might tentatively suggest that the influence of surrealism—no less prominent in the L.A. of Nathaniel West—also accounts in part for this distance. But it is a distance enforced at least as much by the offscreen dialogue, the music and the *choice* of subjects as it is by the images themselves. Doggedly anti-Hollywood in its negativity, the film nevertheless becomes no less

ritualistic about its own assumptions—requiring, for instance, that all the heroine's attempts at fulfillment are equally doomed. After attending a wrestling match with an older man named Kirtz (Herschel Bernardi), she is obliged by the didactic plot to stop off with him next at a strip joint, and a subsequent joyless New Year's Eve party is followed just as mechanically by (a) the despair of off-screen sex and (b) the promise of redemption the morning after, accompanied by such images as Judith taking her car through a car wash:

Merrill: It's Sunday morning—
Baxley: I know.
Merrill: You took a shower.
Baxley: Twice.
Merrill: You washed the bathroom, the kitchenette and the ashtrays.
Baxley: Around the clock.
Merrill: Why?
Baxley: I got a thing that won't wash off—the slime of loveless love.
Merrill (with glib finality): Masturbation by proxy.*

Yet ironically, it is the priviliged position assumed by this dialogue—and the corresponding denial of a prominent direct sound that would allow us to listen to the camera's subjects—that makes some of the film's images akin to those in pornography, providing the basis for a kind of aesthetic masturbation whereby the roving "savage" eye becomes an equivalent to the stroking hand. Significantly, the film's most powerful (and climactic) sequence, which immediately follows the above exchange—a faithhealing session conducted in a church that Judith visits on Sunday morning—is the only one in which the music and dialogue vanish, to be more than amply replaced by the sounds of the event itself. Here, for

---

* *All the transcriptions of dialogue in the film used in this article are made by the author.*

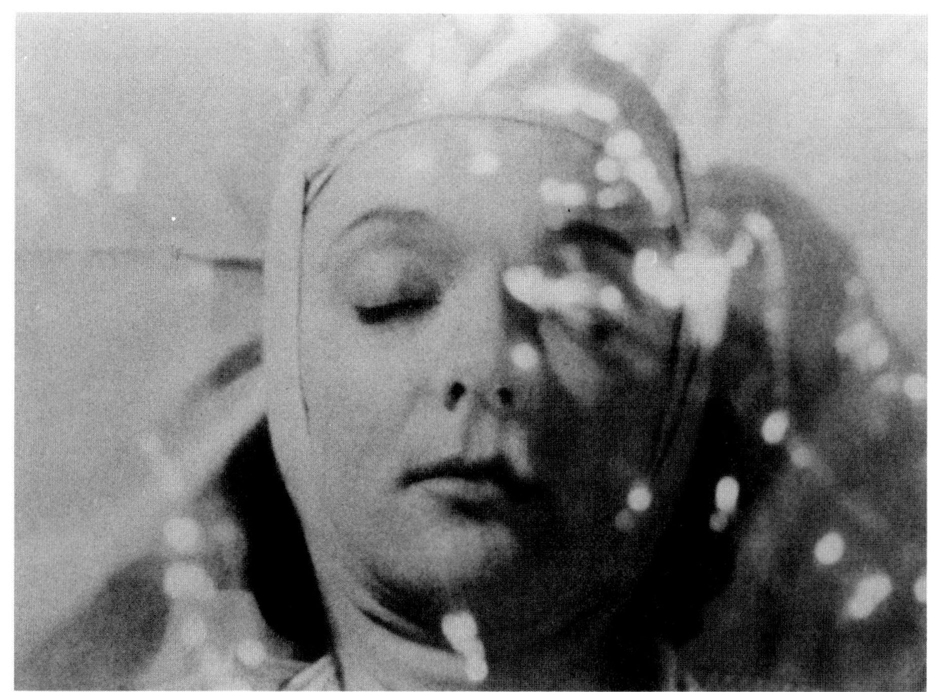

once, documentary triumphs over fiction and poetry, and the corrosive power of the images and sounds—the wailing anguish of faces and voices (mainly female) speaking in tongues and weeping, the droning reassurances of the preachers (all male) offering comfort—confounds any possibility of facile verbal and melodramatic paraphrase, and the film's litany of suffering turns into a kind of aria that clearly needs no support.

Here and here alone, the effect towards which the entire film has been aiming is fully and devastatingly achieved in all its complexity, illuminating the religious context that is elsewhere evoked principally through the over-heated dialogue. By contrast, the belated feelings of universal love expressed by Judith after she survives a freeway accident (e.g., "His candle burns for me"; "We're all secret lovers of one another") seem contrived and false, an unconvincing "New Testament"

postscript to the dispassionate "Old Testament" implacability which precedes it. ("Could it be that we Americans overvalue Love ritualistically because we under-value it actually?" Dwight Macdonald wondered in his review in the October 1960 *Esquire*.)

One of the most historically interesting aspects of *The Savage Eye* today is the degree to which it seems both ahead and behind its own time in relation to modernism. While the commentary and score tend to remain just as dated and as "moderne" as they were in 1960, the iconographic surface of the film and certain other aspects (including the ethnographic detachment) are striking anticipations of images and ideas which would inform modernism over the following two decades. Set the offscreen voices of Merrill and Baxley alongside those of Godard and Marina Vlady, and the hat store and beauty parlor of *The Savage Eye* (among other settings and references) become startling approximations of the no less sociologically approached boutique and hairdresser in *2 or 3*

Things I Know About Her. The use of stream-of-consciousness—no less pronounced in Godard's *The Married Woman,* where it is also juxtaposed with sociology—is equally evident. By the same token, the film's fascination with car accidents parallels a comparable obsession in contemporary painting, sculpture and fiction. Even the pitiless voyeurism towards (and through) sex, violence and psychosis seems to echo certain attitudes and preoccupations in such varied writers and directors as Beckett, Buñuel, Burroughs, Flannery O'Connor, Franju, Kubrick, Robbe-Grillet and Nathanael West, while a brief, melodically fragmented atonal piano theme used for dramatic emphasis evokes a similar use of one in Antonioni's *Eclipse.*

By contrast, the overall thrust of *Shadows* is resolutely premodernist—or, at least, modernist only in the sense that Method acting as derived from Stanislavsky and Chekhov continues to be modernist. Here, however, it is difficult to be authoritative, for we are essentially dealing with the second of two versions of *Shadows,* and the only one that has been available since 1960; and the earlier version was widely celebrated by Jonas Mekas as the superior *and* more modern of the two, a film whose relative rawness and lack of structure made it a significant early example of the New American Cinema. According to letters by Cassavetes and Carruthers which appeared in *The Village Voice* on December 16 and 30, 1959, the first version was screened at midnight at three successive non-admission screenings at the Paris Theater, attended by a total of about 2,000 people. Eight additional scenes were then shot for the second version after the first failed to acquire a distributor, and according to most accounts, the major change in the editing was an increase in continuity and conventional narrative structure. By necessity, we can only deal here with the second version—a document which is itself of major importance in the American cinema as a whole, and which has been woefully unknown to most Cassavetes fans for far too many years.

A few words need to be said about the film's inception. Cassavetes and director Bert Lane had organized a dramatic workshop held in a studio with a stage. One night, apparently, the late-night radio talk show announcer Jean Shepherd visited one of their sessions and was especially impressed with an improvisation which took place between actors, during which a young man (Tony Ray, the son of film director Nicholas Ray) discovers that his girlfriend (Goldoni) is black when she greets her dark-skinned brother (Hurd). Shepherd invited Cassavetes to appear on his show *Night People,* where the latter described his workshop and his desire to film their work if he could raise enough money, inviting listeners to pledge their support. According to Hurd (in an interview with Clara Hoover in *Film Comment*), $2500 was raised within a week's time. (The final cost of the release version was estimated at around $40,000, and Cassavetes later remarked it was "three years in the making." *The Savage Eye,* which cost $65,000, required four years of work over weekends.) And once started from this encouragement, the film grew as a collective improvisation out of the scene that Shepherd had witnessed.

Shadows' improvisational method and collective authorship are as closely linked as these attributes are in subsequent films co-signed respectively by Jacques Rivette and Robert Altman; so it is scarcely surprising that group interactions and intimacies of various kinds— between family members, friends, couples and associates—quickly become the very subject and substance of the film. *The Savage Eye,* on the other hand, essentially rejects the group for the individual or the abstraction (sociological or poetic), and the overcomposed commentary makes the film—for all the documentary immediacy of much of its footage—seem like the reverse of improvisation.

A crucial distinction must be made about the films' immediate impacts and the different standards of judgment that these impose. Thanks to the brilliance, attractiveness, humor and courage of such actors as Hurd, Crosse, Goldoni, Ray and Carruthers, it is possible (and often tempting) to love *Shadows* for its flaws as well as its triumphs, much as one can admire the risks and wayward inspirations of the best jazz players. Considering the subtle yet crucial fact that the film's racial theme is scarcely alluded to at all in the dialogue, although it is frequently central to the action, an extraordinary amount of sensitivity and vulnerability permeate these rare performances.*

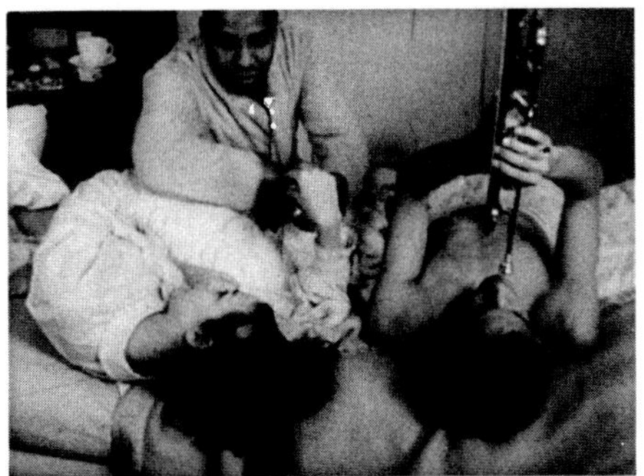

Signs of this range from effective cornball Method riffs—like Tony pausing just a beat between two words in his seduction of Lelia ("You've got the softest lips I've ever . . . felt")—to subtle interplay between Hugh and Rupert, so delicately and sweetly nuanced that it becomes a veritable lesson in ways that people can behave decently towards one another. (At the other end of the spectrum is the crude, anti-intellectual bullying assigned to Lelia's hapless writer friend David Pokitillow, whose improbable "literary party"—a satire of sexual come-ons, coverups and cultural pretentions which would eventually lead to much finer observations in Cassavetes' *Faces*— is equally unconvincing.)

Regarding the incestual feelings that are touched upon in the siblings' scenes together, it is easy to be reminded of J.D. Salinger's Glass family, another team of neurotic New York actors. But the warmth of Cassavetes' family goes much further—past racial barriers and class snobberies, and without specious references to clichés of suffering humanity like the Fat Lady of *Franny and Zooey* (who surely belongs more in the menagerie of *The Savage Eye,* along with the suicidal Buddy Glass). The mutual affection shown between Hurd, Goldoni and Carruthers (and between Hurd and Crosse, where the closeness is almost familial) is a potent ingredient in all their scenes together, and winds up surviving every other social bond in the film— including that of Bennie and his white pals Dennis (Sallas) and Tom (Allen), whose aimless exploits with women frame the main action of the film, and whose cohesion seems to dissolve at the end, after they lose a brutal fight with another male trio, returning Ben to his loneliness.

This sense of human closeness, recalling at times the ambiance of early Truffaut films made around the same period, culminates in the long scene staged on and around Lelia's bed—where the two brothers become virtual rivals for her affection—and the final visit paid to their flat by Tony, just as Lelia is leaving with a black date. This leads to a reversal of roles between Bennie and Hugh, with the former suddenly becoming the voice of tact and reason as he decorously gets rid of Tony—a beautiful scene of dawning recognition where Tony's own square form of repentance becomes the catalyst for the brothers' own mutual expressions of love and forgiveness. It is at such moments (and there are others) that *Shadows* shows its true documentary colors—creating and recording its own kind of love on the screen.

Jonathan Rosenbaum is the author of *Moving Place: A Life at the Movies* (1980) and a contributor to *Artforum, American Film, Sight and Sound* and *Omni.* He has taught film criticism at the University of California at San Diego, New York University and the School of Visual Arts.

Pull My Daisy The Queen of Sheba Meets the Atom Man

J. Hoberman

Gregory Corso *Pull My Daisy*

"I don't see how I can review any film after *Pull My Daisy* without using it as a signpost," wrote Jonas Mekas in *The Village Voice* after the half-hour movie had its New York premiere—on a Cinema 16 doublebill with *Shadows*—in late 1959. Comparing *Pull My Daisy* to the Living Theatre production of Jack Gelber's *The Connection* (soon to be filmed by Shirley Clarke), Mekas asserted that both works "clearly point toward new directions, new ways out of the frozen officialdom and midcentury senility of our arts, toward new themes, a new sensibility."

More than any previous American avant-garde film, *Pull My Daisy* was the product, if not the manifesto, of an official avant-garde movement. Based on the third act of Jack Kerouac's unproduced play *The Beat Generation,* the film was narrated by Kerouac, lensed by the Swiss-born photographer Robert Frank (whose epochal collection *The Americans* had just been published, complete with Kerouac introduction), and directed by Frank and the abstract expressionist painter Alfred Leslie. Whereas *Shadows* arrived upon the scene almost unheralded, *Pull My Daisy* had already garnered a fair amount of pre-screening publicity. Indeed, the filmmakers had even taken out an ad in the April 15, 1959 issue of *Variety* extolling *Pull My Daisy* as "a splendid entertainment for the entire family—no sex—no violence."

A few weeks after its New York premiere, *Pull My Daisy* was cited in a *Life* magazine feature on America's new rebels, and was written up in *Time* ("Zen-Hur") a month later. It was the year of the beatnik—after several seasons of increasing notoriety, Jack Kerouac and Allen Ginsberg were virtually household words, Roger Corman set his drive-in cheapster *Bucket of Blood* in a Venice, California espresso joint populated by jive-talking hipsters, Albert Zugsmith cribbed a title from Kerouac, dubbing his latest Mamie Van Doren vehicle *The Beat Generation* while another Hollywood studio undertook a film version of Kerouac's novel *The Subterraneans.* Small wonder then that, back in New York, a group of Wall Street investors led by Walter Gutman and Jack Dreyfus were prepared to risk $25,000 or so on a 35mm amateur film featuring the real Beats.

From *Pull My Daisy:*

Peter Orlovsky, Larry Rivers, Allen Ginsberg, Gregory Corso

Sally Gross, Alice Neel, Mooney Pebbles

Peter Orlovsky, Gregory Corso, Allen Ginsberg

Larry Rivers, Delphine Seyrig

The stars of *Pull My Daisy* include poets Allen Ginsberg, Gregory Corso, and Peter Orlovsky, painters Larry Rivers and Alice Neel, and a young French actress (who had come to New York to study the "method" and was being featured in her first film role), Delphine Seyrig. The film's cast and crew encompassed several bohemias and—like the painters' theater (or happenings) that began to appear around 1958-59—*Pull My Daisy* now suggests the culmination of various post-war aesthetic trends in acting, painting, music, and poetry that variously proclaimed improvisation, spontaneity, and "emptiness" as their hallmarks.

For the most part, *Pull My Daisy* is a series of antic doings in a Bowery loft (actually Leslie's Fourth Avenue studio). Sweetly self-aggrandizing, the film is a celebration of a certain lifestyle—here personified by Ginsberg, Corso, and Orlovsky (who play themselves), as well as Rivers (enacting a railroad brakeman named Milo). Kerouac describes the film's action, speaking for all the characters in a humorous and grandiloquent monologue that's interspersed with sound effects and music by David Amram. Frank's studiedly casual compositions emphasize the minutiae (and mild squalor) of loft living, punctuating the interiors with occasional, poetic cutaways to the street.

Although *Pull My Daisy* is sometimes described as "plotless," it does follow a relatively linear narrative, encompassing a single day and restricted to a single setting. Awaking ("early morning in the universe"), a character known only as the Wife (Delphine Seyrig) makes breakfast for her young son (Pablo Frank) and hustles him off to school. As the boy goes through the door, two friends of her husband, Ginsberg and Corso, come tumbling in. More or less ignoring the Wife, the duo amuse themselves by declaiming poetry, drinking wine, smoking pot, clowning around, and falling out. Eventually, Milo—the man of the house—returns from work, Peter Orlovsky in tow.

The Wife's genteel aspirations and latent squareness become apparent when she informs Milo that she's invited the Bishop over for afternoon tea. The Bishop, who looks about 20 years old and is accompanied by his sister and mother (Alice Neel), is thoroughly confounded by the unruly poets, most memorably when—after a discussion of Buddhism—"Peter the Saint" demands "Is baseball holy?"

Are alligators holy?" As a freeform jam session begins, and the child, Pablo, reemerges in his bathrobe, the Bishop and his entourage retreat from the loft in confusion. The Wife then loses her temper ("all the time we give them wine and beer . . . all these beatniks in the house") and starts to cry. Milo, in turn, gets angry and storms out into the night with his feckless friends, treating them to an exhibition of tapdancing on the stairs.

Pull My Daisy won a prize at the San Francisco Film Festival in 1959 but was unable to attract any commercial distribution until Emile de Antonio, then an architectural consultant, took on the task as a labor of love. In April 1960, the film opened theatrically at Dan Talbot's newly established repertory house, the New Yorker, on a bill with *The Magnificent Ambersons.* Shortly after, *Film Culture* presented its Second Independent Film Award (the first having gone to *Shadows*) to *Pull My Daisy:* "Its modernity and its honesty, its sincerity and its humility, its imagination and its humor, its youth, its freshness, and its truth is [sic] without comparison in our last year's pompous cinematic production. . . It breathes an immediacy that the cinema of today vitally needs if it is to be a living and contemporary art."

However, despite *Film Culture*'s enthusiasm (and the fact that such normally conservative critics as Dwight Macdonald and Bosley Crowther had kind words as well), *Pull My Daisy* was by no means unanimously appreciated by the partisans of avant-garde film. Maya Deren attacked the whole notion of "spontaneous" filmmaking, likening *Pull My Daisy* to "an amateur burglar in a strange apartment, turning all the drawers on the floor, cutting up the mattresses, ripping the backs off pictures, and in general making one ungodly, clumsy mess in a frantic search for a single different note." From another perspective, critic Parker Tyler—who contrapuntally praised *Shadows*'s "casual directness"—called *Pull My Daisy* "a designing improvisation," "arty," "*recherche*" ("the scene witnessed by the camera eye . . . is as old as the location of the Provincetown Theatre"), and "as fresh as a frozen green pea, which, of course, in a manner of speaking and after all, is an authentic green pea with a relatively new unfreshness."

As an observer, Tyler proved more astute than Deren. Ten years after *Pull My Daisy* was conceived, Alfred Leslie published an article in *The Village Voice* debunking the notion of the film as a "spontaneous documentary," a term used by his co-director Robert Frank. Addressing himself to "the persistent misbelief that *Daisy* is either 'cinema vérité,' spontaneous, or improvisational film," he explained that the movie was "no more random or improvised than Antonioni or Rossellini." According to Leslie, "the set was dressed . . . Copies of the script were made for the cast. Suggestions were made as to what to wear. A shooting schedule was planned . . . Each scene was marked and slated. Each scene was rehearsed and shot three times."

The most cherished myth regarding *Pull My Daisy,* put forth by Mekas and others, is that Kerouac created the narration off the cuff, in a kind of "intoxicated trance." Actually, by Leslie's account, Kerouac "did the narration four times, once at home in Long Island, to 'get the feel of the footage,' and then three times in a sound studio a few months later. The last three narrations were cut, edited, and rewoven into one track."

In short, the extreme informality which characterized *Pull My Daisy* was a deliberate and sophisticated aesthetic strategy. (Leslie, after all, was an action painter who once polemically produced two identically splattered canvases.) Before long, though, the film's provocative apparent spontaneity was dated and surpassed by the crudity of the films Mekas would call the "Baudelairean cinema."

"As *Shadows* and *Pull My Daisy* marked the end of the avant-garde-experimental cinema tradition of the 40s and 50s (the symbolist-surrealist cinema of intellectual meanings), now there are works appearing which are marking a turn in the so-called New American Cinema—a turn from the New York realist school (the cinema of 'surface' meanings and social engagement) toward a cinema of disengagement and new freedom," Mekas reported in the May 2, 1963 issue of *The Village Voice.*

The films to which Mekas was referring were Jack Smith's *Flaming Creatures,* Ken Jacobs's *Little Stabs at Happiness,* Jacobs's and Bob Fleischner's *Blonde Cobra,* and Ron Rice's *The Queen of Sheba Meets the Atom Man,* "four works that make up the real revolution in cinema today." These movies, Mekas wrote, "are illuminating and opening up sensibilities and experiences never before recorded in the American arts . . . a world of flowers, of evil, of illuminations, of torn and tortured flesh; a poetry which is at once beautiful and terrible, good and evil, delicate and dirty."

Like *Pull My Daisy,* the movies cited by Mekas were "pad films," depicting nonconformist, boho lifestyles in a picturesque slum milieu. However, the films of the Baudelairean cinema diverged from *Pull My Daisy* in several important respects. One, they were far more raw—shot in hand-held 16mm rather than 35mm, using outdated film stock and readymade soundtracks. Two, they were far more explicit—filled with male and female nudity, "queer" behavior, and blasphemous references to the American popular culture of the 1930s and 1940s. Socially, these

films were at once more outraged and more outrageous than *Pull My Daisy.* As Tyler would observe, the latter was "*in*authentic from the newer viewpoint . . . because it shows bohemian life as the *artist's* life;" the protagonists of *Blonde Cobra* or *The Queen of Sheba Meets the Atom Man*, by contrast, were less visionary poets than performing madmen. In other words, while *Pull My Daisy* presented the beat generation's upper crust, the films by Rice, Jacobs, et al plumbed its lower depths.

Ron Rice, the most explicitly "beat" of the Baudelairean filmmakers, was born in New York in 1935. A high school dropout, he first bought an 8mm camera to record bicycle races. In 1960, Rice drifted out to Squaw Valley, California with hopes of filming the Winter Olympics; instead, he ended up in San Francisco where he met Taylor Mead and made a 75-minute film called *The Flower Thief.* A coffeehouse poet (and former stockbroker), Mead here played a sort of Zen village idiot, clutching a teddy bear as he wandered through the fleshpots of North Beach. *The Flower Thief* was haphazardly constructed and filled with non sequiturs—the beatnik film *par excellence*; Mekas would later praise its post-*Pull My Daisy* aesthetic, including "the utmost disrespect for the 'professional' camera, plot, character conventions."

The Flower Thief had its New York premiere in April 1962 at Cinema 16. Three months later, Rice was named "most promising filmmaker" at the Charles theater's first Filmmakers Festival where he was represented by *The Flower Thief* and his disjunctive Mexican travelogue, *Senseless.* Shortly afterwards, *The Flower Thief* opened theatrically at the Charles (a rundown rep house on the Lower East Side) and received something close to a rave review from *The New York Times* critic Eugene Archer. Meanwhile, Mead—whom *The New Yorker* would subsequently describe as "a cross between a zombie and a kewpie [who] speaks as if his mind and mouth were full of marshmallow"—became the first underground movie star. Rice immediately embarked upon his most ambitious film, *The Queen of Sheba Meets the Atom Man,* starring Mead in a mad scientist variation on his *Flower Thief* persona.

Even more than in *The Flower Thief,* Mead's spontaneous shenanigans are the subject of *The Queen of Sheba.* He first appears stumbling out of bed—sock-hat covering his ears, tongue and fingers aflutter—rubbing his hands with vaseline. After completing these ablutions, Mead goes to his decrepit kitchen and attempts to cook up some "heroin" before a huge barrel of the substance crowns him. Subsequent scenes show Mead strolling by the Central Park reservoir (a Chaplinesque derby balanced precariously on his head), slobbering over the model of an atom at the Union Carbide "World of the Future," or posing idiotically in front of various modern artworks at the Guggenheim Museum.

Playing opposite the diminutive "atom man" is an enormous, seemingly tipsy, and frequently naked black woman, Winifred Bryant. Although in the film's most lyrical sequence Bryant makes a solitary trek across the city— walking through Central Park, riding alone in an elevated train, floating across the icy harbor on an apparently empty ferry—she mainly serves as the goodnatured foil for the regressive, manic Mead (and, later, Jack Smith). Bryant has some hilarious scenes, dallying with a young white boy who she flings around her colossal breasts as though he were a rag doll, but *The Queen of Sheba* is Mead's movie. When he clambers out of a closed trunk—festooned with confetti, wearing diving flippers, licking a football, and rubbing up, dog-like, against the air—it's to establish the outer limits of aimless, impulse behavior.

In early 1963, Rice screened excerpts from *The Queen of Sheba* at the Living Theatre. "This is a wild mad rough cut like no *Hollywood* director would show the public for fear of having his ideas stolen," he bragged in the program notes. "We defy anyone to cop our style. This is only 70 minutes of a protracted [sic] 3 hour epic by the director of *The Flower Thief.* This is your opportunity to help challenge the Hollywood stranglehold on morals, expression, and art and what have you. Dig us." The screening was intended to be a benefit for the film but Rice took the money raised and the next day flew to Mexico. Although he came back to New York later in the year to make *Chumlum*— an impressionistic short influenced by, and featuring, Jack Smith—Rice never completed *The Queen of Sheba.* He soon returned to Mexico where he died of pneumonia in late 1964.

Supervised by Rice's assistant Howard Everngarm, the 70-minute rough cut of *The Queen of Sheba* was placed in distribution with the Film-Makers' Cooperative. Some 15 years later, Taylor Mead edited another, longer version of the film, complete with soundtrack, which he maintained was closer to Rice's original intentions. But even this can only be seen as a succession of individual shots. As Fred Camper observed in a review of the Everngam version, "One finds it hard to believe, given the complexities of *Chumlum* and *Senseless,* that had Rice completed the film entirely as he wanted to, he would not have created some of the hallucinatory confusion of all his individual other films."

Thus, like Sergei Eisenstein's variously reconstructed *Que Viva Mexico, The Queen of Sheba Meets the Atom Man* as we have it is very much a hypothetical film. Along with Jack Smith's abandoned *Normal Love,* Ken Jacobs's unfinished *Star Spangled to Death,* and Andy Warhol's dismantled ****, it is one of the lost masterpieces of the period—a victim, in a sense, of its own commitment to immediacy.

J. Hoberman writes weekly film reviews for *The Village Voice* and is a frequent contributor to *American Film* and *Artforum.* He is a filmmaker and co-author with Jonathan Rosenbaum of the forthcoming book, *Midnight Movies.*

Nothing But A Man
The Cool World

Noel Carroll

Hampton Clanton *The Cool World*

Egalitarianism was one of the greatest, if not the loudest, concerns of the 60s. America, it was discovered, was an unequal society. The recognition of this fact came as a shock to many, and served as a rallying point for innumerable social, political and personal agendas of the period. Along with general recognition that not everyone was treated equally, there was also a specific recognition that not everyone was heard equally. That is, the established culture—TV, movies, indeed the whole complex of what came to be called mass media—did not represent the whole compass of the American experience even-handedly. A typical TV series—more likely than not— would have as a central character a white, middle-class male, though many viewers were neither white, middle-class nor male. Gradually, in the 60s, such phenomena came to be regarded as exclusionary, and as a form of cultural domination. As the decade wore on, the battle for representation had not only a political dimension—as blacks struggled for voting rights—but a further cultural dimension as different groups aspired for equal representation not just in the legislatures but in the media as well.

Much of the activity of the American independent film movement is best comprehended within the context of the mounting battle for cultural representation. It strove to confront the dominant cinema on a series of issues, both in terms of style and content. It presented subculture, counter-culture, beat-culture and minority culture versions of the American scene, presupposing the necessity of representing these viewpoints as a crucial means of enfranchising other-than-mainstream variations on our national experience. This process is unmistakably in operation in the cases of *The Cool World* and *Nothing But a Man,* both "problem"-oriented films that try to depict aspects of the black experience with more realism and more of an "inside" understanding of black life than would be found in even the ambitious, socially conscious ventures of the dominant media such as *To Kill A Mockingbird.* That film, for example, grapples with the problem of racism in a way that filters the issues through the point of view of a white girl-child and the heroic actions of her Lincolnesque father.

The black civil rights movement was the first of the great, post-World War II egalitarian revolutions; in many ways it was the model for the movements to follow. In the early 60s, the civil rights movement was marked by the nonviolent tenor sounded by Martin Luther King, and it was devoted to achieving equality between blacks and whites through due process of law. The rhetoric of the movement was grounded in simple justice, claiming for blacks only that which most whites already had. Both *The Cool World* and *Nothing But A Man* bear the pre-

Watts and pre-Black Power stamp of this stage of the civil rights movement. Their form of address is not that of the firebrand or the revolutionary; neither film threatens retaliatory black violence. Unlike a film such as *The Harder They Come,* both works are underwritten by the hope that the documentation and explanation of injustice will move people of good will to eradicate it. These films suggest neither revolutionary upheaval or violent apocalypse but instead try to show, in the case of *The Cool World,* how discrimination leads to the needless waste of lives mired in brutality and violence, and by showing, in the case of *Nothing But A Man,* how racism causes conditions in which self-destruction and cruelty flourish.

Both *The Cool World* and *Nothing But A Man* are "theme" films, dedicated to expounding an idea by means of a dramatic narrative. The particular idea, which both films explore, is the notion that racism creates a set of circumstances in which blacks themselves inflict a great deal of the misery they suffer upon themselves; part of the invidiousness of racism is that it turns the victim into his own executioner. In *The Cool World,* this thesis is worked out through the experience of the adolescent, would-be gang leader, Duke, whose limited world view—the product of segregation—is dominated by the belief that to be a man and to gain respect is to have a gun and to be a real, cool killer. Pursuing this mythic ideal of selfhood, of course, has the direct consequence of harming other blacks. Duke's violent ethos guarantees suffering for other blacks, and, ultimately, for himself. In *Nothing But A Man,* the indignities of racism force the central character, Duff, to turn inward and to sour. His frustration turns into self-hatred and begins to smolder into cruelty toward his saintly wife, Josie.

Though *The Cool World* and *Nothing But A Man* are propelled by simple ideas, neither feels like a tract nor veers into the self-explanatory preachiness or staged dialectics of a *Guess Who's Coming to Dinner.* Both films avoid overt, summary statement—thereby distinguishing themselves from the facile, Hollywood, race-problem film—and they elaborate their message by dramatic implication. They try to capture a sense of the psychological processes that bring about some of the generic phenomena that shape the contours of everyday black existence. The films achieve this by means of their plot structures. Both films are developmental in design; both chart the evolution of the consciousness of their central, male characters. In both films, this involves the characters' awakening to the fact that they are enmeshed in self-destructive psychological traps. In *Nothing But A Man* the process of awakening is gradual, distributed evenly at several stations along the way of the plot's progress. In *The Cool World,* the awakening comes abruptly, hitting Duke like a ton of bricks in a series of untoward events that erupt back to back as the film hurries into its finale. In neither film is it clear what practical value these awakenings will have for the characters in question. At the end of *The Cool World,* Duke is manacled in a police car, on his way to another beating and probably a jail sentence, though he is now suddenly aware of the futility of the macho-gunman creed. In *Nothing But A Man,* Duff and Josie embrace; Duff knows he must not alienate himself from Josie; but there is no answer to the question of how he can work with dignity for The Man. Neither film advocates a definite program for responding to the problems of racism. Both concentrate their energies on revealing the psychological traps racism conjures up for blacks. The awakenings that the films dramatize are, in a manner of speaking, necessary preparations for

confronting racism, but they are not themselves such confrontations. The awakenings Duff and Duke undergo are the fictional correlatives to the audience's emerging understanding of some of the psychological straits blacks are caught in under racism.

Of the two films, *Nothing But A Man* is the more classically narrated. It builds to its crisis and quasi-resolution by carefully setting out Duff's character against a background of studied foils and contrasting characters. The credits roll by over a stunningly photographed scene of a group of black men laying tracks for the railroad somewhere near Birmingham. These men are gandy dancers. Relatively high paid, they lead a nomadic existence, shuttled to and fro by the railroad wherever repairs are needed. They are a rootless, all-black, cloistered male group, living together for weeks on end until they complete each job. Like soldiers, the workers brag of their freedom, yet to outsiders their nearly monastic way of life appears exploited, oppressive and claustrophobic. The opening scene in their battered bunkcar is one of edgy tedium; the men loll around with nothing to do but get on each other's nerves. Duff is singled out for special attention when the railroad men head to town for a night out. Rather than taunt a local B-girl in the manner of his friend Frankie, Duff buys her a beer without expecting any sexual favors. Thus, Duff is marked off as someone different from his fellow workers—someone with a sense of nobility and a commitment to decency which makes him an immediate locus for the audience's allegiance. He leaves the bar and wanders into a church service which presents an alternative style of life— one based on family, responsibility and religion. Though the very

opposite of his own, rough *modus vivendi,* Duff is attracted. He meets Josie, a school marm and the preacher's daughter, and he wants to see her again.

Their courtship is initiated by symmetrical scenes of disapproval. Duff's friends ridicule him, suggesting that his prospects for sexual fulfillment with the likes of Josie are pretty low, and worrying that Duff wants to give up the freedom of the road for the half-life of domesticity. In suit, Josie's parents warn her of the dangers of the wild, no-account sort of man that gandy dancers are reputed to be, and her stepmother snidely insinuates that there's just one thing that could interest Josie in Duff. Josie and Duff obviously see each other as natural complements. Josie is an antidote for Duff's rootlessness while Duff has vitality and courage, uncommon virtues among the house-broken, middle-class black males Josie knows. The two want to forge a new kind of life, one that falls between the options of either the footloose loneliness or repressed domesticity that surround them. But it is not clear that society-at-large will allow blacks to survive outside these two stereotypes.

The love affair is beset with difficulties from the outside. The impossibility of reconciling domesticity and dignity becomes increasingly frustrating to Duff, and his only recourse appears to be to regress into rogue malehood. As his anger grows, it spills outward. Isolated, Duff can only assuage his pain by hurting Josie; but that is only another way to hurt himself. Duff is aware that racism is effectively dehumanizing him, and, concluding that he is "no longer fit to live with," he leaves in a gesture that seems meant to explain the break-up of many black homes. He goes to Birmingham where he visits his father for the second time in the film. Will's deterioration since their last meeting has been precipitous. The old man is in an interminable drunken stupor, shouting at Duff to leave while his mind founders. He has become a mass of human wreckage and waste, even more pathetic because much of the torment is self-made. Duff tries to rush his father to the hospital, but the old man dies in the car. While making funeral arrangements, Duff is brought face-to-face with the testament of the rogue male. No one knows when or where Will was born, or what work was his specialty when he was alive. In the book of life, Will was a desolate, blank page. Reading this as a premonition of his own fate, Duff is once again

Abbey Lincoln, Ivan Dixon
Nothing But A Man

quickened into action by his father's negative example. He retrieves his own son, James Lee, and returns to Josie, their final clutch symbolizing Duff's determination to give himself roots through the family. The camera holds on Josie's tearful face. She is, at first, crying for joy. But there is anguish too, perhaps because she realizes that though Duff promises that everything will be alright, they have still not discovered a way of really reconciling Duff's role of domestic breadwinner with his righteous desire for self-respect. Indeed, if there were one criticism that might be leveled at the plotting of *Nothing But A Man,* it would be that the emotionally satisfying reunion of Duff and Josie blurs the audience's recognition that the major problem developed by the narrative—the incompatibility of sustaining a black household and maintaining one's self-esteem—has not been resolved. Nevertheless, on the asset side, the film does clearly demonstrate how racism causes frustrations that can turn one against oneself and those one loves. And this certainly is the sort of knowledge that can be emancipatory.

The classical plotting of *Nothing But A Man* is matched by its generally conservative cinematic style. This, however, is not a criticism since, though often conservative, the cinematic qualities of the film are of an especially high caliber. Shot in black and white, at a time when this had come to connote serious intent, the filming stresses strong contrasts rather than softly mapping the grey scale. This prompts a feeling of austerity and even harshness which appropriately coincides with the bare settings, underscoring the sense of indigence. Producer-cinematographer Robert Young has a special flair for shooting work and machinery. Using low-angle shots and often capturing action simultaneously on two visual planes, Young monumentalizes labor, imbuing the track laying, the trip to town on the handcar and the milling with heroic stature. One derives not only a sense of the physicality and communality of work from Young's brief portrayals, but a sense of strength and definition as well. Group acting is also handled scrupulously though not perhaps with understatement. Many scenes require—in the same shot—shifting attitudes from the players: Rev. Dawson, for example, smiles when the white school superintendent makes a dubious witticism, but then signals displeasure when the man turns his back. These dramatic touches are framed perspicuously, and the

overall strategy of handling dramatic ensembles in this way is an effective means for conveying the disparity in perspective between what the generally insensitive whites think is going on and what we know the blacks think of them.

For the most part, *Nothing But A Man* is an independent film that shows little of the influence of the formal innovations of the French New Wave, or of the vibrant American experimental movement of the early 60s. Except for its stylistic asceticism—which I tend to think its creators still would have imposed for expressive purposes even if they had had a bigger budget—*Nothing But A Man* is not constructed that differently from a studio film. It is basically comprised of dramatic scenes which are set out efficiently, sensitively, but classically. However, in what might be thought of as the film's interstices—the material *between* the dramatic scenes (e.g., Duff's travels to and about Birmingham)—one does see evidence of the new styles of 60s filmmaking. Primarily, this involves the use of documentary-type shooting—including apparently hand-held cameras—of the sort associated with cinema verité. A good example of this is the panning of the congregation when Duff comes upon the church meeting. The shooting, because of its style, looks like an extract from a nonfiction film of the period (and, undoubtedly, the black and white photography enhances this effect). This imitation of documentary forms in a ficition film format not only evinces a 60s interest in what was thought of as mixing documentary and fictional modes, but also performs a useful rhetorical function in this film of social criticism since it operates to claim some kind of documentary "authenticity" or "honesty" for itself by dint of its cinema verité look. This expropriation of the connotations of the ostensible veracity of nonfiction technique continues to this day with famous examples such as *Battle of Algiers* and certain scenes in *Mean Streets* and *The Deer Hunter.*

Whereas *Nothing But A Man* limits its forays into vanguard documentary stylization to its interstices, *The Cool World* has a rough, spontaneous-looking, cinema verité appearance throughout. The camera is hand-held, the black and white film stock is fast, scenes are obviously shot on location rather than on sets, and the boys are nonactors playing themselves with a nod to Italian neo-realism. As well, a great many details of Harlem street life, that have little direct bearing on the narrative, are packed into the montage, giving the film an undeniable aura of being steeped in—being in the thick of—its subject. Again, the documentary look and putative direct-cinema spontaneity that this fiction film imitates give it an expressive purchase on the kind of veracity and contemporaneity that cinema verité promoted. Of course, any spectator looking at this film for more than a few minutes can figure out that it is not an unstaged documentary. Nevertheless, in its exploration of the use of documentary techniques in a fiction format, the film betrays an early 60s obsession with realism, one that

held that cinematic virtue, if not truth, lay in recording the way things were as closely as possible. In retrospect, we see that much of the conceptual foundations of this ethos were misguided—there is no correlation between wobbly camera movement and epistemological certainty. However, at the same time, it is hard not to catch the urgent feeling, and desire to capture the moment that is anxiously inscribed in the improvisatory mannerisms of cinema verité (especially when that style is contrasted to that of either the contemporary TV documentary or studio drama of the 60s). In adapting the cinema verité style, *The Cool World* makes itself appear hip, in touch with its subject, savvy, up-to-date, intimate and in-the-know while speaking directly. You could call it a case of virtue by association.

Apart from the qualities of "authenticity" that its style projects, *The Cool World* is also notably consistent in engendering a feeling of abruptness. Many shots end with flash-pans. In all probability, this was done to make editing easier. But it prompts an atmosphere of nervous tumult and of rapid, chaotic transitions. It makes this brutal world feel even more unsteady, full of wrenching changes that can come at any time. As well, the film often straight-cuts from scene to scene rather than fading, thus exacerbating its abrupt quality. If the classical style of *Nothing But A Man* is appropriate for its rural, Southern setting, *The Cool World* is a nervous, jagged, Northern urban nightmare, tossing fitfully from shot to shot and scene to scene. The musical score, hard jazz that punctuates the film in often short jabs, heightens this feeling as does the narrative which does not prepare the audience for what comes next but drops us into many successive scenes as if we were *in media res* time and time again.

Before preparing this essay, I had not seen *The Cool World* for fifteen years. Upon re-seeing it, I was very much impressed by its formal rigor, and its brilliant editing and sound mixing. The film is an intricately crafted artifice which is designed and minutely controlled to provoke the impression that it is an artless slice of life. Its tempo is magnificent, blending the directionless pulse of hanging-around time—the unemployed boys are on vacation—with the sharp transitions, across several dimensions of the exposi-tion, which mirror the contingency of the boys' social world, a place where violent and abrupt changes are the order of the day. One technique that recurs throughout the films seems to me especially distinctive. Often when Duke is wandering around the street, even when we hear his voice-over thoughts, the editing includes cut-aways to everyday street scenes: couples, children, dogs, storefronts. These shots are often very difficult to fit into the story. They don't seem to be point-of-view shots, i.e., shots of things Duke is looking at; nor are they simple establishing shots in the normal sense of the term. Uncon-nected directly to the narrative, they seem to almost float into the film, shards of facts related to, but unfet-tered by, the story. At first, you might think that their function is to universalize the story—to imply that what is being said of Duke could apply to all of Harlem. But the images seem too fugitive and disparate to add up to a general comment. They provide atmos-phere, of course. Yet, it is the way they are situated in the film that makes them special. For these "floating facts" seem randomly placed, accentuating the slice of life effect, and, perhaps more impor-tantly, conveying a feeling of aim-lessness (where "aimlessness" is a specific condition in the narrative that gives rise to the self-destructive life style of boys like Duke.)

The film begins with three incisive scenes stressing the segregation of blacks in American society. First we see an abrasive close-up of an incensed black orator—a man as angry as Ras The Destroyer in *The Invisible Man.* As the camera pulls back, giving us a wider, shaky, cinema verité catalogue of street scenes, often connected by flash pans, the imagery—with inserts of policemen and a plaster-cast Jesus—bears out the preacher's claim that whites are an intrusive, invasive force in Harlem. In the next scene—after Duke meets Priest who offers to sell him the gun that obsesses the boy for the rest of the film—Duke and his friends pile onto a school bus for an educational tour of Wall Street on which their cranky white teacher badgers them every inch of the way. The camera details the trip downtown at length. It is impossible to miss the gradually emerging contrast between the tattered poverty of Harlem and the increasingly grander appointments of the white sections of Manhattan. This scene is not just a travelogue of New York. It literally measures the distance of Harlem from the financial center of the city which, needless to say, also comments on the "distance" of blacks from the white center of power. The scene establishes that Harlem is unequivocably separated, physically and economically. These high school kids are crossing a geographical border into a foreign land. In the third scene, the boys' distance and segregation from the American Dream is given pictorial embodiment. In the background of a shot, we see the statue of George Washington in front of the Treasury Building; the white teacher pronounces a civics lesson in front of it. But in the foreground of the shot—palpably on a different, lower, visual plane—we see Duke and his friends chattering away, oblivious to the teacher. They are not part of

the world that belongs to Washington, Wall Street and the teacher. They are outside, in a realm of their own, divided, segregated and apart, not merely in space, but, as the film comes to emphasize, in consciousness as well.

Suddenly, on an abrupt cut, the film leaves the white world and plunges into Duke's. Compressing time and space, the film presents two hectic scenes: Duke snatches a purse which, in turn, he loses to a rival gang, the Wolves, who beat him insensate on his own stairway. Both the action and the cinematic presentation define this new world as violent and full of threat from every direction. Duke is carried up to his parents' apartment, but he staggers to his feet and sneaks out as soon as they are asleep. This is an important moment in the film because it underlines that Duke is separated not only from the white world but from the world of adults in general. This point is most strongly stated when Duke's friend, Littleman, drives his own father from his apartment with a knife, and the boys turn the flat into a clubhouse. From then onwards, though Duke returns at times to his parents' home, Duke lives essentially in a world of adolescent ritual and fantasy, unchecked by any adult reality principle. Part of the power of *The Cool World* is its deft recording and close observation of the rituals and ambience of the adolescent gang. Had the film been made in the era of Black Power, it might have attempted to turn the street folkways of these boys into black virtues, in the manner of, say, *Sweet Sweetback's Baadasssss Song.* But, as it is, the insularity of the boy's world, instead, is developed as a crucial factor in a cautionary tale of self-destruction.

Though the plot seems stitched together episodically—with what follows what in time as its only organizing principle—two questions are woven through the

narrative in a way that pulls the story forward. These are Duke's preoccupation with securing a gun for the rumble, and his desire to overthrow Blood, the ineffectual junkie who leads The Pythons, the gang Duke belongs to. As Duke stalks the streets, selling joints and shaking people down, to get the $50 for the gun, we often attend his thoughts which he speaks in voice-over commentary. His fantasies are extremely repetitive; we are struck by the limitation of his imagination, fixed upon the gun, the gang and getting "fame" by becoming a real, cool killer. His inability to come up with $50 is a poignant enough comment on his limitations. But ultimately more distressing is his compulsive, fixated, incantory, comic-book take on the world which, though it first scares us, finally becomes a sign of Duke's helplessness. As we are uncomfortably locked into listening to Duke's myopic monologues, Duke is locked into the threadbare myth it espouses. We realize that this sort of macho-fantasizing can survive only as long as it remains contained in the world of adolescent ritual; as soon as it crosses into the space of the real world, however, there will be trouble. The "cool" in the film's title is fraught with pessimistic irony.

The film offers Duke very few options. The only positive alternatives he has are represented by a friend of Duke's, a basketball player presumably headed for a scholarship, and Blood's brother, a freedom rider. But these characters are sketched too briefly to seem like real alternatives for Duke. Instead, his options are narrowed to Blood, who Duke says taught him what he knows, and Priest, who also adopts

a mentor role toward Duke. But his is a choice between the devil and the deep blue sea. Blood is a wasted drug-addict, and the dapper Priest gets a bullet in the head for all his smartass shenanigans, as Duke appears to realize in an agonized moment toward the end of the film.

Duke almost recognizes in time that he is on a disaster course. These murmurings of self-knowledge come through his affair with LuAnn, a child prostitute who services the Pythons. She has poetic dreams of escaping her sordid surroundings which seem to move Duke, albeit incoherently. The couple goes to Coney Island, but LuAnn disappears inexplicably. The psychological effect on Duke is marked but unclear. It, at least, takes his heart out of the upcoming rumble. He's on the verge of giving it up. But events move too quickly upon him. The rumble ensues, and he is involved in the meaningless killing of one of the Wolves. Duke runs to the clubhouse, only to find Priest dead there, a harbinger of his own fate. Duke runs home, but the police grab him, beat him and drag him off in a furiously paced, inescapable and brutal exercise of real world justice.

The overall sense one has at the end of *The Cool World* is that of needless pain. In some ways, it could be compared to *Raging Bull,* a film in which the central character destroys himself because of his lack of understanding and his adherence to an obsolete, ethnic, macho creed that comprehends the world solely in terms of fast fists. *Raging Bull,* like *The Cool World,* is the story of self-destruction through monumental ignorance, through living in a fantasy that has little connection with the actual, surrounding world. *The Cool World,* however, differs from *Raging Bull* by locating Duke's adolescent view of the world and his lack of a reality principle in a social context. For Duke's self-destructive fantasies, which all but guarantee a wasted life for him, are the product of *de facto* segregation, and the insularity it creates. If Duke lives in a dangerous psychological dreamworld, the economics of the actual world has brought this about. As the film ends, there is mention of the Constitution, a document we often associate with equality. But in this context, the allusion is bitter. For it comes at a moment when we recognize that America, a country that literally brags about its egalitarianism, is in fact anything but an equal society. Yes, Duke is given a certain legal equality under the Constitution. But when it comes to what could be significantly called equality of opportunities, *The Cool World* has shown, through its combination of anthropological observation and psychological insight, that those equalities are something that Duke has not got.

From *The Cool World*:

Carl Lee, Hampton Clanton

Carl Lee (left)
Hampton Clanton (center)

Yolanda Rodriguez,
Hampton Clanton

Noel Carroll teaches philosophy at the School of Visual Arts, New York. He is the co-editor of *Millennium Film Journal* and a contributor to *Dance Magazine.*

Babo 73
Hold Me While I'm Naked
Hallelujah the Hills

Richard Peterson

Peter Beard *Hallelujah the Hills*

The Surrealists of the 1920s were avid cinéastes, and they particularly admired the short comedies of Mack Sennett, Charles Chaplin, and Buster Keaton for their spirit of spontaneity, incongruity, and irreverence. This appreciation went beyond a simple elevation of popular culture in defiance of the standards of "fine art." To the Surrealists, these comedies fostered a potential liberation from conventions: gags of surprise could bring the irrational into play, and the films' debunking of authority figures could suggest a critique of the social order.

Some of the Surrealists' own films appropriated techniques from these comedies without adopting the idea of a comic hero, such as Chaplin's tramp or Keaton's stoic, as a mediator of the comic event or as a protagonist with whom an audience could identify. In *Un Chien Andalou* (1928) and *L'Age d'Or* (1930), Luis Buñuel eschewed the concept of audience identification and used comic juxtapositions in order to transgress religious and social taboos to the violent extreme that Andre Breton would later term "black humor."

With the exception of James Broughton and Sidney Peterson, comic sensibilities emerged infrequently in the early years of the American experimental film. Filmmakers from Maya Deren to Stan Brakhage proposed an analogy between film and poetry as a legitimate alternative to the formulaic "prose" of Hollywood cinema. As the filmmaker's consciousness progressively became the subject of his own work, performance in a traditional sense—that is, concerning an actor who assumes a concrete role—seemed to be one of the cinema's outmoded conventions of illusion.

Hallelujah the Hills (1963), *Babo 73* (1964), and *Hold Me While I'm Naked* (1966) are comedies in which the filmmakers recognize and acknowledge multiple traditions: silent comedy, as well as its extensions into sound through the Marx Brothers and W.C. Fields; the Surrealist mobilization of comedy's anarchistic impulse; Hollywood convention and cliché; and the formal innovations of American abstract film artists. Their makers are film watchers, and their references to these traditions are wholly conscious and playful. Each film is an episodic narrative with concrete characters, although to varying degrees, the performers are called upon to maintain distance from their roles. They don't conceal the fact that they are acting.

Citing the parallel explorations of Happenings and Pop Art in the plastic arts, critic Parker Tyler wrote that one of the most significant achievements of the Underground film emerging in the late 1950s was its "recognition of the value of the film work as charade." (Parker Tyler, *Underground Film: A Critical History,* Grove Press, 1969, New York) Performance in these three films is dominated by a sense of play, and the success of the comedy lies, to a great extent, in the actor's ability to share the enjoyment of play-acting with the audience.

The value of play is both substance and subject of Adolfas Mekas' *Hallelujah the Hills.* One of the first commercial successes of the Underground cinema, this is an art film that is also a parody of European art films, and as such, it summons another body of work into its canon of cinematic references: the films of the French New Wave, especially those by Alain Resnais, Francois Truffaut, and Jean-Luc Godard. *Hallelujah the Hills* is an open-ended, demonstratively lyrical story of a love triangle set in rural Vermont. Jack (Peter Beard) and Leo (Martin Greenbaum) both love Vera, who is played by two actresses (Sheila Finn and Peggy Steffans) in order to represent each man's image of the "ideal woman." From the very beginning, Mekas establishes the whimsical nature of this story's telling. Intertitles, like those in a silent movie, introduce the characters in posed portraits. We are immediately informed that the grotesque Gideon has already won Vera, and the body of the film traces, in non-linear fashion, the previous seven years of Jack and Leo's courtship. As in Resnais' *Last Year at Marienbad* (which is pointedly satirized in one scene), the dramatic resolution is inconsequential; we're along for the tour.

Athletic Jack visits Vera and her parents every winter; Leo the aesthete surfaces in the summer. The men appear to spend the rest of the year camping, hunting, and playing in the woods. Mekas constructs two levels of comic detail: the individual eccentricities of his characters and his own manipulation of the scenes through sight gags and magical juxtapositions. Jack may pilot both front and rear of a fallen tree that he and Leo are transporting across our line of vision, or he may notice the rectangle that the camera lens has superimposed over his car. Along with cinematographer Ed Emshwiller, Mekas structures the narrative according to the rhythmical spirit of each scene, rather than its dramatic weight.

Hallelujah the Hills is a film about the romantic fantasies of men. Vera exists primarily in terms of Jack's and Leo's imaginations, and our own perspective on these young men is suffused with their self-images. Mekas portrays the male/male and male/female relationships in different ways. The courtship scenes are often staged and edited with spatial and temporal discontinuities that convey each man's ultimate inability to "connect" with Vera. During Jack and Vera's winter walk, as the camera fragments their trajectory by tracking repeatedly past them, the film launches—as though it were Jack's wish fulfillment—into the ice-flow scene from *Way Down East* (1920), directed by D.W. Griffith, the cinema's great "connector" of both narrative space and idealized lovers. In contrast to the elliptical quality of Vera's scenes, the relationship between Jack and Leo is depicted in a simpler manner. The camera often observes them passively, affording them the time and space in which to improvise their games.

In *Hallelujah the Hills,* play is the most successful means of communication. However, Jack and Leo's playful existence has a grave irony. While Mekas celebrates the spirit of their unconventional behavior, he also exposes its underside. In the opening scene of the film, a camera iris (suggesting a spyglass as much as silent film convention) opens on the

unidentified pair toting guns and directing their jeep through the woods. Charades of the hunt and military maneuvers abound in their relationship during the off-seasons, when they are not "stalking" Vera or competing as rivals for her love. Jack echoes both motifs in two distinct scenes in which he feigns death: first as a fallen animal in its spastic death throes, and then as the casualty of an imaginary aerial attack on a military graveyard.

Like children, they immerse themselves in fantasy to the extent that they are blind to the implications of their games. In an existence of total pretense, their freedom is illusory. Just as they never can complete their profession of love for Vera, they will never be complete themselves. Their displacement at the end of the film by another pair of child-men is justified thematically by their ultimate inadequacy.

The two convicts who complete the film with its final shot (in both senses of the word) provide a perfect closure to the interrelated themes of game-playing and death. Played by Taylor Mead and Jerome Hill, they are visually reminiscent of the infantile convicts that Laurel and Hardy portrayed in the silent film *Liberty* (1929). Like Laurel and Hardy, they appear to be convicts only by virtue of their striped uniforms (which may well be pajamas, since we encounter them sleeping by the side of the road). With puny weights chained to their ankles, these grotesque versions of Jack and Leo bicker over a pair of duelling pistols before playing the final game. "Let's do it," says Hill. "I can't count," replies Mead, who turns conspiringly to the camera and adds, "I'll shoot first."

Boys will be boys.

Laurel and Hardy
Liberty

Jerome Hill, Taylor Mead
Hallelujah the Hills

Taylor Mead
Babo 73

Taylor Mead, James Greene
Babo 73

The boys who cavort throughout *Babo 73* present a greater threat, because they are running the country. Robert Downey's film is a hipster's *Duck Soup*—political satire rendered as comic-book caricature. Its patchwork structure of blackout sketches and improvised tableaux is propelled by Downey's relentless pursuit of the absurd. The characters' names signal pure farce: Sandy Studsbury, ineffectual "President of the United Status," Chester Kittylitter, his academic "left-hand adviser," Laurence Silversky, the hawkish "right-hand adviser;" and Green, the Presidential secretary undergoing a nervous breakdown. Even the title of the film is a touch of Dada: is it a vulgarization of "Babel" or is it only a "foaming cleanser"?

Downey produces black humor by staging this bureaucratic decay as though it were a Cold-War minstrel show. "Hubba, hubba, hubba!" sneers Tom O'Horgan's soundtrack chorus at the beginning, as an insane priest assaults a hitchhiking woman. One-liners are dispensed constantly in shotgun-fashion: Kittylitter touches Silversky's coat and asks, "Is that Black Muslin?" and Silversky greets his associates with a cheerful "Bomb 'em!"

In Downey's vaudeville show, the establishment's "straight men" are wholly interchangeable. Kittylitter clarifies his liberal stand on Civil Rights by referring to his tome "The Negro as Diabetic," and the camera tilts down to a shoeshine boy at his feet. Throughout the film he covets Silversky's combat boots, and when he does get them, he also assumes Silversky's right wing ideology.

The narrative outline on which Downey builds his sketches concerns the particular day that Studsbury and his advisers await the arrival of Snodgrass, a white "peace-poet" who has been beaten brutally while attempting to register at an all-black college. In the course of this eventful day, they launch a nuclear war that is intercepted by God and receive progress reports about the Red Siamese takeover of the East and West coasts.

Individual sequences are uneven in effect, but Downey's strongest directorial strategy is his employment of actual street locations in New York and Washington, D.C. The juxtaposition of his characters, dressed in business suits and gesticulating wildly, against the background of the White House or U.N. Plaza gives many sequences the gritty texture of street theater. The central strength of the film, however, is Taylor Mead's performance as the President.

Mead, who literally burst onto the screen in *The Flower Thief* (1960), Ron Rice's ode to the "Beat" sensibility, is the best comic actor that the Underground cinema produced. He brings to his diverse roles a pre-adolescent innocence reminiscent of a classic comedian like Stan Laurel, yet maintains effortlessly the kind of modernist distance that would please the avant-garde filmmaker who rejects the illusion of traditional character. Unlike Laurel's rhythmical gestures that were polished in the music hall, Mead's body language has an arhythmical, almost spastic quality of emotional abandon. As P. Adams Sitney observed in an early appreciation, Mead's stylized activity on an open street, no matter how staged, ". . . appears natural because one has the feeling that Taylor Mead himself would do this sort of thing." (P. Adams Sitney, "The Sin of Jesus and The Flower Thief," *Film Culture* No. 25, Summer 1962)

The best moments in *Babo 73* recall the picaresque strategies of *The Flower Thief,* presenting Mead in improvisational activities in public areas. Leading his staff in calisthenics on a game field, he loses coordination and falls down. Carrying a small American flag close to his heart, he quietly marches past a double row of parking meters and salutes them as though they constituted a military review line. He directs a huge missile carrier as though it were backing into his garage.

At an actual military parade, filmed in the style of television news, he stands by a car filled with real generals. The tentative fiction of his status as "President" makes his solitude in this crowd rather poignant. A couple of the officers smile at this patriotic "character" who carries a toy flag, and as the military vehicle rolls away, he gently waves to them—and they wave back. The scene is magnificent in its "live" quality. Mead's comic presence is so natural that he can absorb actuality into his own playful fiction. What the President tells his advisers at the end of *Babo 73* applies to Mead's performance: "I think it's been a very creative day; I think we've come up with some classics, a few beauties . . . a masterpiece."

The mock grandeur of *Hold Me While I'm Naked* begins with a triumphal musical fanfare, a barrage of colored lights, and a field of shooting stars bearing the actors' unfamiliar names. George Kuchar addresses Hollywood modes more directly than any other avant-garde filmmaker. The conventions of exotic melodrama appeal to him for their excesses as well as their genuine pleasures. The films that he and his brother Mike have produced since their Bronx, New York childhood have titles of exaggerated vulgarity: *Corruption of the Damned, Sins of the Fleshapoids, Pagan Rhapsody,* and so on. For all their intended hyperbole, however, George Kuchar's miniature melodramas are much more than "camp" parodies.

In *Hold Me While I'm Naked,* Kuchar himself plays a filmmaker of low-budget exotica whose attempts to direct his actors' nude scenes are constantly frustrated. This diminutive mogul shouts instructions with the vigor of a von Sternberg: "Okay, now take off the brassiere . . . because the mysticism of the stained-glass window and the profanity of that brassiere don't go well together." The actors in the film-within-the-film ignore him or drop out of the production as they become immersed in "real" sex play.

Hold Me While I'm Naked is a meditation on the gulf that exists between subject and object in the act of filming. Kuchar's character projects absolute earnestness in his work, and the distance between his aspirations and his ability to realize them makes his loneliness poignant. Like Taylor Mead, but in a more controlled and "directed" context, he paints a sympathetic portrait of the "innocent" as outsider.

As the director of *Hold Me While I'm Naked,* Kuchar demonstrates a formidable command of Hollywood film language with which he can both engage and subvert our expectations of narrative tensions and resolution. His comic vision can absorb particular gestures of the avant-garde, as in the scene in which a burst of laboratory marks on the film seems to make his character rub his eyes. However, his power as a filmmaker lies in his commitment to structure and the way that he mounts the most incongruous material with an elegance reminiscent of Alfred Hitchcock or Douglas Sirk.

His cinematography emphasizes the sumptuous colors of the Mexican rug, blue shower curtain, or pink bedsheets that decorate the run-down Bronx apartments, and he fills every scene with the most emotive soundtrack music that Hollywood has to offer. After his "wrap" on the love scene involving the stained-glass window, the camera embarks on an extended tracking shot of his character taking a thoughtful walk through the woods. The camera is fixed on his face, from a low vantage point with a wide angle lens that distorts his features. The soundtrack music is lush and romantic but suddenly becomes suspenseful in tone, even though Kuchar has not changed the visual information of the scene. Playing with our emotional expectations of such a mechanism, Kuchar exposes the clichés of Hollywood melodrama by elaborating on its techniques.

With the exception of his own character, all of the performers in the film overact, and their stylized gestures are emphasized further by the dubbing of exaggerated Bronx accents and cartoon-like foreign accents. Hollywood kitsch pervades even these characters' private lives. The leading lady begs her Latin lover to take her where she will be appreciated for more than her body, and the leading man walks out on one of Kuchar's phone calls for a hallway rendezvous with a "femme fatale" dressed in black. In the grand finale, Kuchar intercuts each couple's lovemaking in the shower—acted with the sensual abandon of a DeMille bathtub scene—with his own character revolving absurdly in his shower, banging his head in frustration against the wall of pink tile. The majestic orchestral music finishes on the image of fragile television antennas trembling as the snow falls outside his window.

Kuchar's film is more than Hollywood parody, because he consciously explores the dichotomy between his great craft and the economic means he has to exercise it. As we consider both, Kuchar's hero becomes not only a figure with whom we can identify, but the point of departure for a larger critique of film form. Like Mekas and Downey, he is aware of the conventions of Hollywood narrative film and its traditions of film performance. All three filmmakers subvert these conventions through modes of play. While Mekas constructs his story like a Chinese puzzle and Downey fires a barrage of improvisations, Kuchar takes the bold measure of burrowing through the conventions from the inside and then pushing them beyond their limits.

Donna Kerness and friend
Hold Me While I'm Naked

George Kuchar
Hold Me While I'm Naked

Richard Peterson has been film
curator at Walker Art Center
since 1979.

Come Back, Africa
The Brig

James Roy MacBean

A penny-whistler in *Come Back, Africa*

Come Back, Africa by Lionel Rogosin, and *The Brig* by Jonas Mekas: here are two films, each associated with the American avant-garde of the early 1960s, which creatively defy categorization. And here are two films which, in startlingly original ways, combine formal experimentation with incisive social observation and provocative political comment.

The film *Come Back, Africa* has always been something of a mystery to me. I had never heard of it, or of its director, Lionel Rogosin, when I first came across a listing for it in the film catalogue at San Francisco State University, where I was teaching in the early 1970s. The catalogue listing told me only that the film was made in 1959; that it depicted the trials and tribulations of a Black South African obliged to leave the tribal homeland to seek work in Johannesburg; and that the film included a wide variety of scenes of "street music" filmed in and around Johannesburg.

I was curious enough to want to see *Come Back, Africa*. So I scheduled it for an open date in my "Film and Society" class. When the lights went up after the class screening of *Come Back, Africa,* I took a deep breath, stunned by the intensity of the film, especially by the raw force of the film's final scene.

On one hand, the plot—with its inexorable series of setbacks—seems open to the charge that it is heavy-handed and contrived. And the ending, Zacharia returning home from his 10-day jail sentence (for violating the pass laws by spending the night with his wife at her new work-site) only to discover that his wife had just been strangled by an intruder, seems blatantly melodramatic and especially heavy-handed. Nonetheless, the all too schematic and potentially cliché-ridden narrative somehow works, and is rendered "authentic", not only by our sense (which I, having lived in Southern Africa, can substantiate) that the characters and events depicted are fairly representative and plausible, but above all, by the remarkable naturalness and touching individuality of the lead character, Zacharia, and of his wife, Vinah. The director of *Come Back, Africa* has achieved a remarkable *intimacy* with his actors . . . or non-actors, as the case might be.

For all the rough edges of the narrative, *Come Back, Africa* is quite a moving film. Moreover, the episodic, disjointed narrative—itself a loosely strung series of vignettes—is held together by a tough thread of documentary observation of the sights and sounds and social contexts of the throbbing, pulsating street-life of Johannesburg and its surrounding Black satellite towns.

Above all, along with the remarkable intimacy and naturalness of Zacharia's characterization, *Come Back, Africa's* documentary sensitivity to the importance of music and the rhythmic movements associated with tribal dance in the everyday life of urban South Africa is especially striking. In fact, *Come Back, Africa*, for all its reliance on fictional narrative conventions, can also be considered a documentary, not only of the general social situation of Blacks in South Africa, but also, in a more specialized sense, as a study in filmed ethnomusicology, documenting the many varied forms of musical expression of urban Blacks in South Africa, and documenting as well the social contexts and functions of those forms of musical expression.

There are work songs, with their cadenced call-and-response patterns so useful for coordinating unison work (even if the work was coordinated for the profits of the white bosses). There are brass bands for the street parades accompanying Baptist weddings, the wedding party boogeying along the main street of Sophiatown, one of the Black satellite towns outside Johannesburg. There are groups of men gathering in rubble-strewn vacant lots to improvise on a kettle drum and enact a tribal dance. And everywhere there are kids with penny-whistles, as the flutes are called—some kids barely old enough to walk, others in their teens, all blowing away, sometimes alone, often in groups, egging each other on with their multi-part harmonies.

And, interestingly, there are scenes of street-corner music filmed right in the white business center of Johannesburg, with lunch hour crowds of whites gaping quizzically, seemingly uncomprehendingly, at the groups of black kids with penny-whistles jiving together for the fun of it, but also for the small change occasionally thrown their way by an appreciative (or perhaps merely patronizing) white onlooker. Then, too, there are shots, a bit disorienting, of one streetcorner group of black kids with guitars aping an Elvis Presley tune ("Teddy Bear"), which they sing, with all the familiar Presley vocal mannerisms, in Zulu dialect. And there are other shots, equally disorienting, although in an opposite sense, of a group of men, in tattered clothes (one man sporting a mangy-looking animal skin as a headpiece), enacting a unison dance, seemingly part of a tribal ritual, on the concrete sidewalks of the Johannesburg business district, watched warily by a few curious passers-by.

Far from merely providing a bit of "local color" on the South African scene, these shots of the myriad varieties of musical expression raise interesting questions about the different social functions of Black music in urban South Africa. Tribal music and dance, even when performed in urban settings, offers people an opportunity to be in touch with their cultural roots and to consolidate, socially, a sense of cultural identity, especially when the performance is more for the performers' sense of collective expression than for an audience's appreciation (and possible monetary patronage). But the temptations of commercialization are obviously there even if limited, for the most part, to the hope of picking up small change on streetcorners; although the dream of "making it big," like Elvis, knows no color bar. In this respect, the presence, in *Come Back, Africa,* of Miriam Makeba—who is shown getting up to sing and dance at an informal gathering of a few friends (all Black Africans)—suggests that even commercial success in the international music scene does not necessarily dilute the cultural integrity of the musical material; and that such an example as Miriam Makeba can be a source of pride and inspiration to others.

Nonetheless, the film is starkly clear about what the ordinary black African faces in everyday life in South Africa. Above all, there is the rigid pass system which enables whites to control the movements of every black, moving them around like cogs in the machine of white economic prosperity, using them as a vast reservoir of human labor, but keeping them from the full expression of their humanity, and

keeping them strictly on the fringes of the affluent society their labor makes possible . . . for the privileged minority of whites. Moreover, *Come Back, Africa* makes it clear just how vulnerable is the unskilled or semi-skilled black African in white-ruled South Africa, where you can be fired for looking the wrong way at your white employer, for not calling him or her "Sir" or "Madam" or "Boss," for joining the African National Congress party, or for talking about going on strike (which will also get you branded as a "commie")—all of which happens to the poignant figure of Zacharia in *Come Back, Africa.*

Finally, the film has the rare merit of acknowledging that in a situation of such stress as is put on blacks in South Africa, some individuals will turn to prey on others; that a new guy in town fresh off the tribal reservation will seem an easy mark for the pimps, prostitutes and drink-cadgers at the local "social club"; that teenage boys will beat up a slightly younger kid for the little bit of money he has picked up playing music on street corners; and that a young wife whose husband is away (or in jail on a pass violation for spending the night with her at her new work-site) can easily fall victim to any man who sees it as an opportunity to take advantage of the situation.

And in such a milieu, is it any wonder that, as *Come Back, Africa* shows in a scene of remarkably incisive conversation among a group of friends, some will take refuge in religion (a "colored", of European father and African mother, speaks of feeling like a "bastard" until he was welcomed into the Bahai faith); some will become cynical ("not only is all religion an evasion," says one black South African man, "art is another evasion. What good is it to think of decorating my room if I haven't got a room in the first place?"); and, finally, some, like Zacharia at the end of the film, who have been pushed around and hurt so much by the inhumanity of apartheid, will be gripped by a rage so powerful that it can no longer be held in check, and will explode, either in a futile gesture of isolated violence or in effective, collective action.

Where the circumstances surrounding the shooting of *Come Back, Africa* are concerned, I did read, some years ago, a brief account—that when planning to make *Come Back, Africa*, Rogosin obtained permission to film in South Africa under the guise that it was for a scholarly research project in ethnomusicology. Certainly the story is plausible; and the interest in ethnomusicology is evident in the finished film. And, lest we forget, the situation of oppression depicted in *Come Back, Africa* still exists in South Africa of today—the last white enclave of privilege on the continent that rightfully belongs to black Africa.

59

Like *Come Back, Africa*, Jonas Mekas' *The Brig* hovers on the boundary between fictional and documentary cinema, and creatively defies categorization. This did not stop it, however, from being awarded the Grand Prize for documentaries in the 1964 Venice Film Festival, even though the film is only, or mainly, a documentary in the sense that it faithfully (but creatively) records a Living Theatre performance of Kenneth Brown's play entitled *The Brig*.

The play by Kenneth Brown, as conceived by the Living Theatre group headed by Julian Beck and Judith Malina, recreates life in a military jail, or brig, where ordinary enlistees are incarcerated for their failure to "shape up" and adjust to the rigid discipline of military life. In the brig, that rigid discipline is intensified with a vengeance: the prisoners are under constant surveillance by tough, hard-nosed sergeants who scream orders at them incessantly, march them in double-time around the little "cage" that is the brig, and sadistically taunt the prisoners in an attempt to break them down or to provoke their insubordination, the least hint of which is considered sufficient pretext for physical threats or actual beatings.

As a theater performance, *The Brig* creates a visceral experience in the audience, which, exposed to the relentless noise (of shouted orders, of mandatory responses by the prisoners, of pounding feet and occasional pounding fists), begins to feel physically worn down, trapped, and strained almost to the breaking point in the same psychological space as the prisoners. As a *film*, Jonas Mekas' *The Brig* tries to bring the audience even closer to the psychological space of the prisoners by utilizing a single hand-held camera which, because it gets right into the actual

physical space (the cramped "cage" of the brig) in which the prisoners are put through their paces, makes the audience feel as if they too are prisoners of "the brig."

The hand-held camera lurches violently when the action in the "cage" gets rough, swings jerkily around in double-time step with the prisoners who are forced to run around their cage like rats on a treadmill, and jolts to a halt abruptly when the prisoners pull up short at the white lines on the floor which they are forbidden to cross without asking the sergeant's permission. Moreover, by moving in close on the sergeants when they engage the prisoners in frequent jaw-to-jaw confrontation, the camera, getting right up under the nose or the jutting jaw of the sadistic officer, gives the audience the very visceral feeling of just how intimidating that claustrophobic proximity to one's torturer can be.

This visual aggression (the rough movements and abrasive close-ups achieved by the hand-held camera), coupled with the aural aggression on the soundtrack (the relentless barrage of shouted arbitrary orders and forced responses—"Prisoner Number Three requests permission to cross the white line, Sir!"), ends up both numbing the mind of the viewer-listener and, paradoxically, activating the mind to make the mental step of transforming raw experience (and here it is extremely "raw") into the kind of symbolic experience we expect from art. In short, if Mekas's film of *The Brig* (like the play itself as performed by the Living Theatre) is able to operate at all at the symbolic level, it has to attain this symbolic status in *us,* not through any use of symbols (which it avoids except for stereotypes) but precisely by its relentless and overwhelming *physicality.*

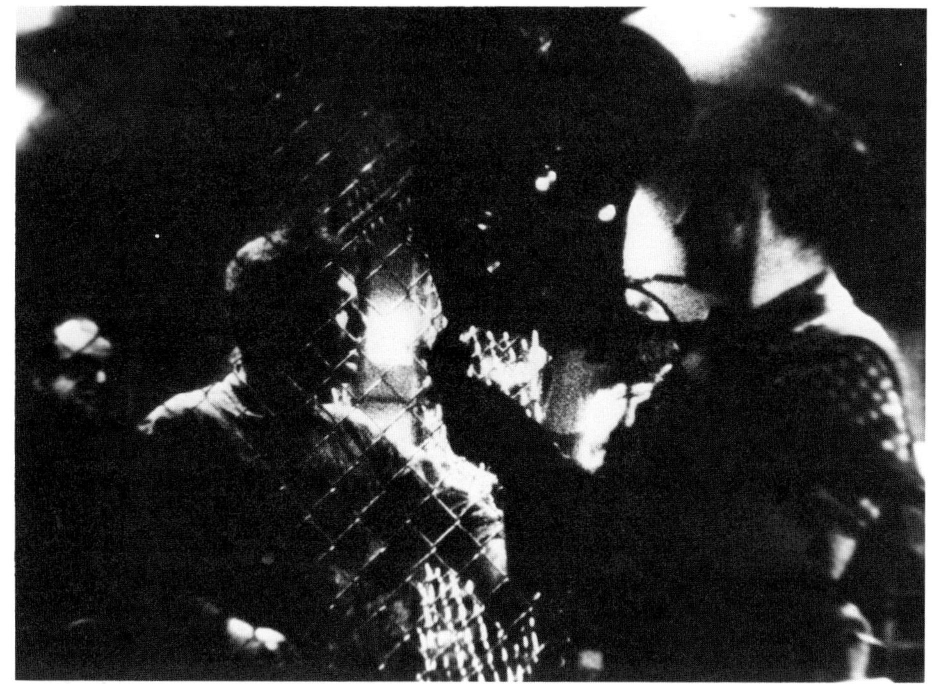

The Brig (film or play) becomes physically and psychologically discomforting in the extreme, thus duplicating in the audience the very sensations of fatigue and stress that would allegedly be the experience of the prisoners of the military brig. Beyond this fatigue and stress, *The Brig* (film or play) seems to encourage us to rise up and rebel against such an outrageously authoritarian and sadistic system as the military is depicted to be.

Some might argue, of course, that *The Brig* (film or play) rests on a fallacious argument; that military brigs are not like (as bad as) this one; and that in any case a military brig is not a fair or accurate metonym (or microcosm) to stand for the military as a whole. One could argue, furthermore, that *The Brig* (film or play) works on the audience in a particularly insidious way that utilizes a guilefully extreme version of what is called in literary criticism, "the pathetic fallacy," wherein the work of art (in this case, the film or play) evokes so powerfully in the audience the same strong emotions allegedly felt by the work of art's protagonists that,

ultimately, the audience no longer sees the work of art as "art" but rather as "real life."

Admittedly, something of this sort has apparently happened in cases where viewers of Mekas' film *The Brig* have not realized it was a documentary of a theater performance and have taken it for a documentary of a 'real' military brig. Such a misconstruing of this particular film also entails the additional misapprehension that documentaries in general are somehow not recognized as works of art making an 'artful' and tendentious *presentation* but rather are thought of as offering an unmediated and immediately credible *representation* of "reality"—a view that is naïve in the extreme (but one which the practitioners, not to mention the viewers of American cinema verité documentaries managed to fall into quite easily.)

One could thus criticize Mekas' *The Brig* (although not the theater performance of the play) for utilizing documentary film conventions which encouraged a naïve belief that what one was seeing was the "real" thing (that is, a documentary of a "real" military brig). And, along this line of criticism, one could add that by also playing heavily on "the pathetic fallacy" and evoking the same emotions in the viewer as the protagonists are alleged to experience, Mekas' *The Brig* (even more than the theater performance of the play) is not as much a symbolic work of art as it is a powerful piece of anti-military propaganda.

On the other hand, one could argue that by creatively mixing conventions from live theater, documentary film and fiction film, Mekas' *The Brig* could possibly lead us to question *all* our conventional sources of "information," at least where the mass media (and theater) are concerned, and to understand as problematic the questionable relations between a work of art and the "reality" it both presents and investigates. All of these issues are complex: and of course they are still very much with us, including, for better or worse, the military and media coverage of the military. Thus it is worthwhile for us to take another look at such a pioneering, powerful and provocative use of the film medium as *The Brig*.

James Roy MacBean is a film critic and frequent contributor to *Film Quarterly* and *Sight and Sound*. He is the author of *Film and Revolution* (1975) which was recently cited as one of the top ten books of the 1970s.

David Holzman's Diary
Portrait of Jason

Wanda Bershen

All you need is love.
The Beatles

Freedom's just another word for nothing left to lose.
Kris Kristofferson

Jason Holliday *Portrait of Jason*

Recollections of the American 60s range from halcyon to grim, depending greatly upon one's age, musical tastes and threshold of tolerance for turmoil; the 60s were everything but dull. Indeed there had been unrest before and the ground for the 60s "revolt" was well prepared throughout the 50s by the Beats in literature and lifestyle as much as by the Cold War and the presence of The Bomb. John Brumfield, in an impressive recent discussion of photographer Robert Frank's book *The Americans* (published in English in 1959), remarks that "for the American pastoralist generally, the world began to slide beyond control somewhere between 1945 and 1947, and by the end of the decade of the 50s, the possibility of a golden America seemed gone forever." (*Afterimage,* Summer 1980). While describing a particular image sequence of Frank's, he goes on to say that "in a society in which identity is a product of cosmetic facility, of self-presentation, life— real, natural, spontaneous life— becomes a contrived fake . . . the search for identity is ultimately a search for a rhetorical stance." Brumfield interprets Frank's book as an "encyclopedia of American alienation" wherein ". . . the landscape is a mirror and it is badly twisted." Finally he points up Frank's central concern with the nature and function of images (art or other kinds), and identifies the Hollywood movie as epitomizing "the media" for Frank's generation, and as representing to them "the absolute nadir of bad faith . . . intoxication, dishonest . . . a microcosm of all that was wrong with America . . . fake life."

What is curious here is the enormous rage expressed towards Hollywood, rightly or not, on grounds of deception. What had changed since the 1930s when Hollywood was internationally revered for its gift of fantasy, even in the midst of a world-wide Depression? Clearly Brumfield reads Frank as chronicler of that spiritual bankruptcy which the Beat writers (Ginsberg's *Howl,* for instance) also struggled with, what has come to be known as the passive, dull, conformist quality of the "Eisenhower Years." His reading reflects as well a sense of outrage and disjunction which should probably not surprise us, since post-war eras rarely find balance and tranquility so easy to achieve as everyone frequently wishes them to be.

Thus we find writers and artists throughout the 50s expressing a sense that indeed the American "landscape" has changed and that what is out there is monstrous. And, like Brumfield and Frank, there was a sense too of incredulity that this could happen, so to speak, in our own backyard. Perhaps it is inevitable that a nation conceived as the utopian dream of the European Enlightenment should have a hard time with the undeniable harshness of being a world power in this most difficult century.

Much to everyone's surprise, what erupted out of the constricted, fearful 50s was a Whitmanesque decade in its insistence upon individual freedom and community simultaneously. The isolated, alienated privatism of everyday life in the 50s was turned on its head, supplanted by a cultural style dominated by what Richard Poirier cannily dubbed "the performing self." (Richard Poirier, *The Performing Self,* Oxford University Press, 1971). The 1960s response to the deeply felt disjunction between "real" life and fiction (that "fake life" attributed to Hollywood and America in general) was a curious inversion—counterculture aesthetics turned everything into theater and the troublesome distinction was neatly obliterated, at least for a while.

Simultaneous with the growth of that counterculture and the development of its stylistic glories and excesses was the emergence of a New American Cinema, analogous as a cultural phenomenon to the rise of Beat literature a decade earlier. This cinema was conceived, too, in opposition to mainstream commercial media, (i.e. Hollywood film and broadcast television) identifying instead with the role and work-style of the individual poet or painter or journalist. It was dedicated to personal and presumably fresh visions, often allied with serious critiques of the prevailing social, political and aesthetic norms. But like the decade in which it blossomed, this cinema was often humorous, witty and irreverent, and above all dedicated to the visionary imagination. Even the documentary works, what became known as cinema verité (or direct cinema), insisted upon a personal rather than scientific or objective approach to their subjects. This movement towards "truthmovies" was in fact the antithesis of the Hollywood canon.

The roster of direct cinema pioneers is familiar now—Drew Associates, the Maysles brothers, Richard Leacock, Donn Pennebaker, Frederick Wiseman, et al. Particular subject matter and stylistic preferences aside, all shared a desire to take an in-depth look at those parts of American life generally deemed unsuitable for media attention. *Warrendale,* Allan King's documentary on a treatment center for emotionally disturbed children and *Titicut Follies,* Wiseman's portrait of a Massachusetts mental institution, were so "realistic" the former was refused broadcast by the CBC, and the latter became embroiled in a long court case which severely limited its distribution at the time. Films like the Maysles' *Salesman* and Pennebakers's music films, *Don't Look Back* about Bob Dylan and *Monterey Pop* about the

California festival in 1967 were less threatening. Verité filmmakers poked into every facet of public and private life in their desire to present the everyday processes within which most of us live, as some counter to the massive myth-making of commercial media. These filmmakers were highly attuned to the ethical issues involved, especially given their emphasis on people talking honestly about personal experiences and feelings. Stylistically some films used more dramatic and narrative structures than others as each maker experimented with whatever mix of camera, directorial and editorial control (or lack thereof) could best achieve his or her purposes. Perhaps the single most unifying aspect of this work in the mid-60s was a felt need to insist upon the importance of everyday people in everyday situations as subject matter at the very least equal to the increasingly glamorized personalities and lifestyles portrayed through mass media. *David Holzman's Diary* and *Portrait of Jason* constitute a lively discourse with the major issues of content and style which verité sought to tackle as well as sharing a concern about notions of documentary "truth" which has been part and parcel of this century's long struggle toward definitions of naturalism, realism, and abstraction in all the arts.

L.M. Kit Carson as David
David Holzman's Diary

Jason, the protagonist of Shirley Clarke's portrait film, is a black, homosexual hustler telling us about a life and a realm of experience definitely not designed to engender viewer comfort. David Holzman, in Jim McBride's diary film, offers a no less disturbing portrait of someone who should be a lot better off than he seems to feel. He is after all, white, male, middle-class and college educated. The latter film raises serious doubts as well about the possibility of establishing anything resembling the nice clear boundaries we all seem to prefer between "truth" and "fiction", personally and cinematically. Both films, albeit in vastly different ways, are demonstrations of that rhetorical creation of a "self" through performance which Brumfield identifies as a long-standing American practice and dilemma. That process, however, reads somewhat differently in the late 60s than it did a decade earlier.

David Holzman's Diary is quite remarkable in its juggling of a central paradox, the fact that neither David nor the film are what they appear to be. From the opening shot we are warned repeatedly about matters of credibility on every level, and the number of viewers who are shocked when the credits come up at the film's end is testimony to a steadfast refusal to mistrust what happens on a movie screen despite massive evidence to the contrary.

The film opens with a brief shot of David outfitted with camera and sound recorder shooting into a mirrored alcove so that what we see is simply not readable as a coherent image. David is in fact double-imaged from the beginning (not to mention the off-screen camera, yet a third player in this drama). In case you didn't get the message visually, David begins by announcing that this is a "fairy tale." The film then cuts to the first extended sequence of the "diary". This shot is set up with three levels of image—the frame as we see it, that framed scene as reflected in the mirror hanging on the wall (center screen)

facing the camera, and within that mirror a second mirror image (from a mirror hanging over the fireplace mantle) reflecting the buildings outside the apartment windows. It is a shot reminiscent of the illusionist play of Velasquez' *Las Meninas,* and equally as conscious and ironic. *David Holzman's Diary* thus announces itself as a story of potentially infinite regress, formally and psychologically.

David proceeds to tell us about his general sense of malaise, having just lost his job and received an A-1 draft classification:
My life . . . seems to haunt me—in uncommon ways. It seems to come to me—from somewhere else. Someone. And I've been trying to understand it; but it seems I can't get it.
(L.M. Kit Carson and James McBride, David Holzman's Diary, *Farrar, Straus & Giroux, New York, 1970)*

He then quotes Jean-Luc Godard's "film is truth 24 times a second" with a mixture of apparent admiration and irony, telling us that he is making this diary film in hopes of "getting" the elusive meaning of his life.

About a third of the way through, a painter friend named Pepe delivers a long monologue on the failure of the Penny sequence (involving David's fashion model girlfriend) the gist of which is that it's not credible and looks like a bad movie. Pepe remarks that in fact neither David nor Penny's life is a good movie. Worse yet he considers this whole diary-movie venture dubious. He describes how the act of filming always changes "reality" and derides the possibility of any spontaneity since David has directed him as to where to stand, how to place the furniture, where he should be in the frame, etc. Finally Pepe accuses David of getting only half-truths which he feels may be worse than a lie. In short, here is the full-dress critique of cinema verité.

The last sequence is sound over a series of still images of David taken in a 25¢ photo booth because all his equipment has been stolen. Fade to black and the credits come up— revealing, of course, the "fraud": that David is an actor, that there was a director and a "real" cameraman.

The point obviously is that a movie is a movie is a movie, that recording and editing are inevitably selective and subjective and will finally reveal what the maker wants it to. But why McBride's severe critique of the "truthmovies"? One is hard put to argue; the film makes a powerful case. In the introduction to the published screenplay, Carson throws out a large hint: "All art's a decoy. Not Real. Not Fact. Not the Truth; but lures you to the Real, the Truth." So, movies are never real, they are sometimes art, and McBride's Truth is very like Godard's, ironic and complex. McBride (much like Godard) offers neither "straight fiction" nor "straight documentary" but a mixture of both, probably a good deal closer to the complex nature of our actual experience and perceptual processes.

Actually *David Holzman's Diary* delivers a good deal of what it promises, not an autobiography, but certainly a portrait. David is a reasonable facsimile of what it felt like to be a draft-age young man in 1967. His sense of unreality, of having no power or control over his life, and of the enormous power of the media environment are familiar. He is not really so different from Arlo in *Alice's Restaurant* (1967) or Dustin Hoffman's *The Graduate* (1968), iconic characters and films of that time. All three are searching, disconnected, unsure of how to relate to the past, present or future, while the "norms" of the adult world

of their parents not only provide no answers, but seem only to muddle the situation.

David's environment mirrors his emotional quagmire—a decaying urban scene, an endless stream of disaster on the radio and television. There are riots in Newark, more horrors in Vietnam, right along with *Star Trek* re-runs, ads for gleaming cars, watches, floor wax and an occasional special event—a demonstration or cops beating up ghetto dwellers. David's obsession with photography was national— stereo components and camera rig were requisite for anyone under 30, while clothes and furniture might be minimal. David is totally equipped (literally and figuratively) with the major communications apparatus of his time but effectively paralyzed, unable to make sense of his world or his life, unable to make the connections with the friends, women or work he seems to want. It's a pretty grim portrait for a decade of so-called liberation— curiously similar to Robert Frank's assessment almost 15 years earlier. There is one major difference. McBride's film seems to point quite clearly to the potential for deception in all media, even when in the hands of a "film artist" rather than the Hollywood dream machine.

Portrait of Jason, a "real" autobiography of a "real" person with a history that sounds more like fiction than truth is surprisingly less grim. Jason is articulate, self-aware in many ways, humorous, and desperate to have our approval. From the beginning we all know that this is a performance, staged for the camera, that it is his big chance to be a star, to be singled out. The film was shot in 12 consecutive hours and the final structure follows the chronology of the shoot. Editing consisted of omitting portions. The film consists of 10-minute reels shot on an Auricon (single-system camera) where the beginning and end of each reel is signalled by fades to white and Jason's image going out or coming into focus. As a result there is virtually no traditional narrative or dramatic structure in the film except for a somewhat climactic ending. Each episode is discrete and our sense of the character is built up through a great deal of what often seems like unrelated bits of information and the sheer amount of time spent with Jason. This is very like the way one actually does come to know people, and very unlike the classic movie, theatrical or literary conventions for creating a character or a story. It is far more like Gertrude Stein's portraits of people built up through the cadence of their speech (and hers) in its non-linear repetition of details and events (cf. Malanctha in *Three Lives*).

We are increasingly amazed that anyone could survive the life of street hustling Jason describes, but he tells the tale with wit and style and even grace. It is not a pretty story nor does he try to justify what he is or what he's done. Perhaps it is that matter-of-factness combined with his enormous need to be liked that breaks down the viewer's inevitable resistance to empathizing with so sordid a life. Confession as a mode in media or literature is tricky (although a 60s staple) but Clarke and Jason handle it well by being thoroughly up front about the whole encounter and the needs it serves for them both.

Curiously *Portrait of Jason* received fairly widespread and positive critical attention, while *David Holzman's Diary* remained largely within the film festival circuit even after winning First Prize at Mannheim in 1967. One wonders why *Jason* might have seemed more palatable at the time. Certainly it is a less convoluted film and does not play upon the viewer's expectations of film, illusion and reality. Also David does not come across as needy, nor does his humor make him attractive. His confusion, depression and narcissism are largely unrelieved. Both protagonists are quintessential anti-heroes and the antithesis of anyone in a Hollywood movie, then or now.

Both films have less to do with notions of documentary or cinema verité than with the issues of representation which have pervaded the artistic, literary and philosophic discourses of the past 150 years. The painter, writer or filmmaker has something in mind which in theory can be presented on a spectrum ranging from highly detailed naturalistic rendering to complete abstraction. *David Holzman's Diary* chooses a reflexive mode of presentation, placing the film in the company of much other film and art, of the 60s in particular, where "real" objects were collaged into paintings, sculptures and assemblages (cf. Rauschenberg's *Bed*) or "real" people replaced actors in Happenings and other new forms of theater. *Jason* takes quite a different tack, electing a "naturalistic" approach. His story is "real," real time and screen time are more or less congruent, and the nature of the event, Jason's performance, is announced at the outset. As subjects in fact, both Jason and David Holzman are entirely within the original art historical definitions of appropriate "realist" content and aesthetics. Speaking of mid-19th century painting Linda Nochlin observes:
. . . Realists placed a positive value on the depiction of the low, the humble, the commonplace, the socially disposessed or marginal . . . turned for inspiration to their own or friends' foyers and gardens, viewing them frankly and candidly in all their misery, familiarity or banality.
(Linda Nochlin, Realism, *Penguin, New York, 1971*)
It is hardly possible here to examine the history of documentary film in relation to the tradition and definitions of realism over the past 150 years, but a few observations are pertinent.

Both these films approach the subject matter Nochlin describes in an explicit and essentially modernist manner. Through direct address in *Jason* and formal structure in *David Holzman,* each signals from the beginning its self-definition as *some kind of performance event.* Similarly, neither film purports to offer us a fixed, immutable reality, but rather a momentary one—that of this encounter, between this chronicler and this subject at this time, no less and no more. Both films are also devoid of value judgments. Unlike earlier realisms they do not attempt to portray the evils of the world nor possibilities for its improvement. Both "stories" are presented with minimal inflection of value about the people or events therein, albeit *David Holzman* is certainly short on patience with the notion of *any representation* (filmic or otherwise) being other than man-made and by definition subjective.

These qualities add up to artifacts which require a fair amount of work from their audience. The viewer must sort through a lot of information and make his or her own judgments as to what is meant, what might be of interest, be germane, or not. Like many other post-war artists, these filmmakers are keenly aware of their historical moment but refuse to moralize or instruct; they prefer to present matters of obvious concern to them and let the audience take it from there.

Inevitably the complex, reflexive kind of realism we might attribute to both films stylistically is linked to major cultural themes. Brumfield discusses this background in remarking on the transition over the past 200 years from "absolutist faith to post-Enlightenment freedom." He goes on to say that if we are removed "from the possibility of moral certitude, one could know facts, but not truth. Meaning had become a matter of relative significance, and the self, once thought to be rooted in an immutable and transcendent soul, was now without stability or foundation."

68

The obsession with identity and with varieties of spiritual belief systems in the American 60s should come then as no surprise. The American version of that search (hardly a new endeavor since belief systems have always come and gone as cultures change) may seem bizarre at times, given the relative youth of this country as well as its size and enormous cultural diversity. But Beats, hippies and now punks are finally not so different from Moonies or the Moral Majority. Each group feels it has achieved some small purchase on a viable identity, and some rules for living.

The two films here do contain some interesting implications regarding the business of identity-seeking. One is that pre-fab personae are no more reliable (possibly less so) than doing-it-yourself (witness the effects of Jason's chameleon act . . .). Both David Holzman and Jason are in fact outsiders due to a combination of circumstance and choice. Each suffers powerlessness and neither, at the point we meet him, seems to feel much ability or inclination to take charge and change things. Both are isolated with virtually no personal or community ties, whereas most action for change in the 60s was taken by people in groups, and the creation of communities to live and work in was a major activity of the decade. Both films thus point up, intentionally or not, the nether side of the traditional American literary or cinematic Outsider—usually a man of honor, of action and often a Westerner. David and Jason are both urban, Eastern, cerebral, verbal in the extreme and consumed only by issues of personal survival. Their performances made public and preserved through recording on film become thus a mode of action, a way to escape isolation, a way to make contact with some audience. The act of *making* these films, as Poirier remarks of his authors' works, is as much the point as the image given of life or living. Such a notion of performance, one which includes the acts of making film, or poetry or music *because* they are the embodiments of positive human energy, is wholly congruent with the aspirations of the American 60s. Performance *assumes* participation, connection, interaction and response—those components of "real" life which were felt to be so sorely lacking in the 1950s artistic and social decorum. Performance is, of course, often unpredictable and you may not get what you wanted or bargained for, but, as the song says, if you try, sometimes, you just might get what you need.

Wanda Bershen is an art historian specializing in media studies including the history of film and still photography. She lives in New York City and works as a film and television producer and consultant for documentary, arts and cultural projects.

| **1958** | **1959** |

1958

Film

Independent
Robert Breer: *A Man and His Dog Out for Air*
Stan Brakhage: *Anticipation of the Night*
Bruce Conner: *A Movie*
Peter Kubelka: *Schwechater*
Shirley Clarke and Willard Van Dyke: *Skyscraper*

Foreign
Andrzej Wajda: *Ashes and Diamonds*
Jean Rouch: *Moi, Un Noir*
Ingmar Bergman: *The Seventh Seal*
Jacques Tati: *Mon Oncle*

Hollywood
Alfred Hitchcock: *Vertigo*
Orson Welles: *Touch of Evil*
Richard Brooks: *Cat on a Hot Tin Roof*
Vincente Minnelli: *Gigi*

The Arts

Visual Arts
New American Painting exhibition tours eight
European countries increasing the international
recognition of abstract expressionists Mark Rothko,
Frans Kline, Willem deKooning and Barnett
Newman.
Happenings begin.
Jasper Johns has his first one-man show at the
Leo Castelli Gallery in New York.

Literature
Harold Pinter: *The Birthday Party*
Vladimir Nabokov: *Lolita*
Lorraine Hansberry: *A Raisin in the Sun*
Jack Kerouac: *The Subterraneans/Dharma Bums*

Music and Dance
John Cage composes *Fontana Mix* for tape. At the
New York School for Social Research he teaches
Allan Kaprow, George Brecht, Al Hansen, Dick
Higgins, Toshi Ichiyanagi and Jackson MacLow. A
retrospective of 25 years of his music is organized
by Jasper Johns, Robert Rauschenberg and Emile
de Antonio at Town Hall in New York.
Merce Cunningham choreographs *Summerspace*.

Political/Social

Economic recession begins in the U.S.,
unemployment exceeds 5 million.
U.S. launches its first satellite, Explorer I, from Cape
Canaveral.
The Beatnik movement, started in California,
spreads throughout U.S. and Europe.
Beginning of widespread use of illegal drugs.
Tension grows over attempted desegregation of
southern schools.
Popular songs include: *Chipmunk Song, The Purple
People Eater, Volare, Catch a Falling Star, A Certain
Smile.*

1959

Film

Independent
Robert Breer: *Eyewash*
Maya Deren: *The Very Eye of Night*
Robert Frank/Alfred Leslie: *Pull My Daisy*
Ed Emshwiller: *Dance Chromatic*
Stan Van Der Beek: *Science Friction*
Stan Brakhage: *Window Water Baby Moving* and
Sirius Remembered
Ben Maddow, Sidney Meyers, Joseph Strick:
The Savage Eye
Lionel Rogosin: *Come Back, Africa*
John Cassavetes: *Shadows*
Film Culture magazine gives its First Independent
Film Award to John Cassavetes for *Shadows*.

Foreign
Robert Bresson: *Pickpocket*
Michelangelo Antonioni: *L'Avventura*
Claude Chabrol: *Les Cousins*
François Truffaut: *The 400 Blows*
Louis Malle: *The Lovers*
Jean-Luc Godard: *Breathless*
Alain Resnais: *Hiroshima Mon Amour*

Hollywood
Alfred Hitchcock: *North by Northwest*
Howard Hawks: *Rio Bravo*
William Wyler: *Ben Hur*
Stanley Kramer: *On the Beach*

The Arts

Visual Arts
Frank Stella produces his Black Paintings.
Robert Frank publishes *The Americans* in English.
Allan Kaprow presents *18 Happenings in 6 Parts*.

Literature and Theater
Norman Mailer: *Advertisements for Myself*
Vance Packard: *The Status Seekers*
Philip Roth: *Goodbye Columbus*
Lillian Hellman: *Toys in the Attic*
William Burroughs: *Naked Lunch*
Ionesco: *Les Rhinocéros*
The Living Theatre presents their production of Jack
Gelber's *The Connection*.

Political/Social

Fidel Castro becomes premiere of Cuba.
C. Wright Mills: *The Causes of WW III*
The Savannah, first U.S. nuclear-powered merchant
vessel, is launched.
Norman O. Brown: *Life Against Death*
Popular songs include: *He's Got the Whole World
in His Hands, Tom Dooley, Everything's Coming
Up Roses, Mack the Knife, Personality, The Sound
of Music, High Hopes.*

1960

Film

Independent
Richard Leacock: *Primary*
Ron Rice: *The Flower Thief*
Stan Brakhage: *The Dead*
Vernon Zimmerman: *Lemon Hearts*
Shirley Clarke: *The Connection*
Bert Stern: *Jazz on a Summer's Day*
Peter Kubelka: *Arnulf Rainer*
The "New American Cinema Group" is formed.
Bruce Baillie forms Canyon Cinema in San Francisco
to screen experimental films.
Film Culture magazine gives its Second
Independent Film Award to *Pull My Daisy*.
Jonas Mekas publishes controversial editorial
"Cinema of the New Generation" in *Film
Culture 21*.

Foreign
Jean Cocteau: *Testament d'Orphée*
Luchino Visconti: *Rocco and His Brothers*
Michelangelo Antonioni: *La Notte*
François Truffaut: *Shoot the Piano Player*
Jean-Luc Godard: *Le Petit Soldat*

Hollywood
Otto Preminger: *Exodus*
Alfred Hitchcock: *Psycho*

The Arts

Visual Art
The *Evening of Sound-Theater-Happenings* at the
Reuben Gallery includes Jim Dine, Allan Kaprow,
George Brecht, and Robert Whitman.
Other Happenings staged by Claes Oldenburg, Jim
Dine and Simone Forti.
Tom Wesselman paints the first of his Great
American Nudes.
Jean Tinguely's *Homage to New York* is shown at
The Museum of Modern Art.

Literature
John Updike: *Rabbit, Run*
Harper Lee: *To Kill a Mockingbird*
Harold Pinter: *The Caretaker*
Ezra Pound: *Thrones* (Cantos 96–109)
Robert Duncan: *The Opening of the Field*
Frank O'Hara: *Second Avenue*
Donald Allen edits *New American Poetry 1945–60*,
an important anthology including Black Mountain,
New York and west coast poets.

Music
Karlheinz Stockhausen composes *Konstakte* for
electronic sound.

Political/Social

Kennedy/Nixon debates televised.
John F. Kennedy elected President of U.S.
Eisenhower tours Latin America.
U.S. U-2 spy plane shot down over Russia.
Civil Rights Act passes giving effective vote to
Blacks.
First laser manufactured.
Popular songs include: *Itsy Bitsy Teenie Weenie
Yellow Polka Dot Bikini, Let's Do the Twist*.
The Twist becomes national dance craze.

1961

Film

Independent
Bruce Conner: *Cosmic Ray*
Jonas Mekas: *Guns of the Trees*
Bruce Baillie: *Mr. Hayashi*
Marie Menken: *Arabesque for Kenneth Anger*
Robert Breer: *Blazes*
Robert Frank: *The Sins of Jesus*
John Cassavetes: *Too Late Blues*
Robert Drew: *Yanki No!*
Film Culture magazine gives its Third Independent
Film Award to *Primary*.
Maya Deren dies.

Foreign
Federico Fellini: *La Dolce Vita*
Karel Reisz: *Saturday Night and Sunday Morning*
Alain Resnais: *Last Year at Marienbad*
Jean Rouch: *Chronique d'un Été*
François Truffaut: *Jules et Jim*
Luis Buñuel: *Viridiana*

Hollywood
Robert Wise: *West Side Story*

The Arts

Visual Art
Exhibition of *The Art of Assemblage* at The Museum
of Modern Art.
Claes Oldenburg opens *Ray Gun Manufacturing
Co./The Store.*
New York galleries, especially Leo Castelli, promote
Pop Art.

Literature
Joseph Heller: *Catch 22*
George Maciunas, ed.: *Fluxus Anthology*
Allen Ginsberg: *Kaddish and Other Poems*
Michael McClure: *Dark Brown* and *A New Book/The
Book of Torture*
LeRoi Jones: *Preface to a Twenty Volume Suicide
Note*
James Baldwin: *Nobody Knows My Name*
J.D. Salinger: *Franny & Zooey*
Henry Miller: *Tropic of Cancer* (first legal
publication in U.S.)

Music
John Cage publishes *Silence*, first anthology of his
lectures and writings.

Political/Social

John F. Kennedy becomes President, creates the
Peace Corps, approves intervention in Viet Nam,
and orders unsuccessful invasion of Cuba at the
Bay of Pigs.
The Berlin Wall erected to stop flow of refugees
from east to west.
Beginning of "Freedom Rides" to test integration
in the South. Freedom riders attacked and beaten
by whites in Anniston and Birmingham.
Popular songs include: *Love Makes the World Go
Round, Moon River, Where the Boys Are, Exodus.*
Bob Dylan produces first album.

1962

Film

Independent
Robert Breer: *Horse Over Tea Kettle*
Ron Rice: *Senseless*
Jack Smith: *Flaming Creatures*
Harry Smith: *Heaven and Earth Magic Feature*
John Cassavetes: *A Child is Waiting*
Albert and David Maysles: *Showman*
Film Culture magazine gives its Fourth Independent
Film Award to Stan Brakhage for *Prelude: Dog Star
Man* and *The Dead*.
Film-makers' Cooperative is founded in New York.

Foreign
Jean-Luc Godard: *Vivre sa Vie*
Michelangelo Antonioni: *L'Eclisse*
Jules Dassin: *Phaedra*

Hollywood
David Lean: *Lawrence of Arabia*
Orson Welles: *The Trial*
John Frankenheimer: *The Manchurian Candidate*

The Arts

Visual Art
Andy Warhol's Campbell Soup Cans, Elvis and
Marilyn paintings shown in first one-man show in
L.A.
Claes Oldenburg has first one-man show, *Store
Days/Ray Gun Theater.*
Pop Art symposium at The Museum of Modern Art.
Time, Life and *Newsweek* feature Pop Art on their
covers.

Literature
James Baldwin: *Another Country*
Aleksandr Solzhenitsyn: *One Day in the Life of Ivan
Denisovich*
Ken Kesey: *One Flew Over the Cuckoo's Nest*
Edward Albee: *Who's Afraid of Virginia Woolf?*
Buckminster Fuller: *Untitled Epic Poem on the
History of Industrialization*

Dance
First performance at Judson Church features
Yvonne Rainer, Robert Rauschenberg, Robert
Morris, Trisha Brown, among others.

Political/Social

Cuban missile crisis.
Mandatory prayer in public schools banned by U.S.
Supreme Court.
Astronaut John Glenn orbits the earth three times.
James Meredith becomes first black student to
register at the University of Mississippi.
U.S. military council established in South Viet
Nam.
Rachel Carson: *Silent Spring*
Marshall McLuhan: *The Gutenberg Galaxy*
Ralph Ellison: *The Invisible Man*
Popular songs include: *Love Me Do, Days of Wine
and Roses, Go Away Little Girl, Blowin' in the
Wind.*
Folk revival in music.

1963

Film

Independent
Kenneth Anger: *Scorpio Rising*
Shirley Clarke: *The Cool World*
Ken Jacobs: *Little Stabs at Happiness*
Gregory Markopoulos: *Twice a Man*
Andy Warhol: *Kiss, Blow-Job, Haircut, Eat, Sleep, Tarzan and Jane Regained–Sort Of*
Ed Emshwiller: *Totem*
George Landow: *Fleming Falloon*
Adolfas Mekas: *Hallelujah the Hills*
Ron Rice: *The Queen of Sheba Meets The Atom Man*
Ricky Leacock and Joyce Chopra: *Happy Mother's Day*
Film Culture magazine gives its Fifth Independent Film Award to Jack Smith's *Flaming Creatures.*

Foreign
Chris Marker: *Le Jetée*
Federico Fellini: *8½*
Ingmar Bergman: *The Silence*
Luchino Visconti: *The Leopard*
Lindsay Anderson: *This Sporting Life*
Alain Resnais: *Muriel*
Jean-Luc Godard: *Contempt*
Tony Richardson: *Tom Jones*

Hollywood
Alfred Hitchcock: *The Birds*
Stanley Kubrick: *Dr. Strangelove*
Joseph Mankiewicz: *Cleopatra*

First New York Film Festival

The Arts

Visual Art
Pop Art exhibition at the Guggenheim Museum includes Andy Warhol, Robert Rauschenberg and Jasper Johns among others.
First exhibition of video art by Nam June Paik.

Literature
James Baldwin: *The Fire Next Time*
Kurt Vonnegut: *Cat's Cradle*

Political/Social

Supreme Court upholds legality of peaceful Civil Rights marches, 200,000 march on Washington.
3,000 troops called out as riots and beatings continue over Civil Rights demonstrations in Birmingham, Alabama. Martin Luther King arrested.
John Kennedy assassinated by Lee Harvey Oswald in Dallas; Lyndon Johnson sworn in as President.
Lee Harvey Oswald shot and killed on live television by Jack Ruby.
Jessica Mitford: *The American Way of Death*
Betty Friedan publishes *The Feminine Mystique.*
Beatlemania sweeps nation. Popular songs include: *Please, Please Me; I Want to Hold Your Hand; She Loves You.*
Joan Baez and Bob Dylan lead in popularity as folk singers.

1964

Film

Independent
Bruce Baillie: *Mass for the Dakota Sioux*
Jonas Mekas: *The Brig*
Ron Rice: *Chumlum*
Michael Snow: *New York Eye and Ear Control*
Andy Warhol: *Couch, Empire*
Mike Kuchar: *Sins of the Fleshapoids*
Michael Roemer and Robert Young: *Nothing But a Man*
Robert Downey: *Babo 73*
Emile de Antonio: *Point of Order*
Albert and David Maysles: *What's Happening! The Beatles in the U.S.A.*
Filmmakers Cinematheque founded in New York.
P. Adams Sitney tours Europe with New American Cinema.
Jonas Mekas arrested for showing *Flaming Creatures* and Jean Genet's *Chant d'Amour.*
Ford Foundation awards grants to 12 independent filmmakers.

Foreign
Peter Brook: *Lord of the Flies*
Richard Lester: *A Hard Day's Night*
Michelangelo Antonioni: *The Red Desert*
Jean-Luc Godard: *Bande a Part* and *Une Femme Mariée*
Michael Cacoyannis: *Zorba the Greek*

Hollywood
George Cukor: *My Fair Lady*

The Arts

Visual Art
Jasper Johns exhibition at the Jewish Museum.
John Cage writes *Jasper Johns: Stories and Ideas* for the exhibition catalogue.

Literature
Michael McClure: *Ghost Tantras*
LaMonte Young: *The Tortoise, His Dreams and His Journeys*
John Lennon: *In His Own Write*

Political/Social

Lyndon Johnson elected President of the U.S.
Martin Luther King awarded Nobel Peace Prize, publishes *Why We Can't Wait.*
Race riots erupt in Harlem, Chicago and other U.S. cities.
Viet Nam war escalates.
U.S. Congress passes Civil Rights Bill.
Free Speech movement begins in Berkeley.
Discotheques with go-go girls become popular. The watusi, frug, monkey, funky chicken and other variations of the twist are the latest dances.
Beatles tour the U.S., appear on the Ed Sullivan show.
Herbert Marcuse: *One Dimensional Man*
Marshall McLuhan: *Understanding Media: The Extensions of Man*
Popular songs include: *Can't Buy Me Love, My Guy, Chapel of Love, A World Without Love, Where Did Our Love Go, House of the Rising Sun, Baby Love, Leader of the Pack, Mr. Lonely, Come See About Me.*

1965

Film

Independent
Kenneth Anger: *Kustom Kar Kommandos*
Ken Jacobs: *The Sky Socialist*
Andy Warhol: 26 films including *My Hustler, Vinyl, Horse, Kitchen, Screen Test*
Stan Brakhage: *The Art of Vision*
Peter Goldman: *Echoes of Silence*
Mary Ellen Bute: *Finnegans Wake*

Foreign
Jean-Marie Straub: *Not Reconciled*
Richard Lester: *Help!*
Roman Polanski: *Cul-de-sac*
Jean-Luc Godard: *Pierrot le Fou*
Jan Kadar: *The Shop on Main Street*

Hollywood
David Lean: *Dr. Zhivago*
Robert Wise: *The Sound of Music*

The Arts

National Endowments for the Arts and Humanities founded.

Visual Art
The Responsive Eye exhibition at The Museum of Modern Art.
New York Theater Rally features performances by Robert Rauschenberg, Jim Dine, Claes Oldenburg, Robert Morris, Robert Whitman and others.

Literature
Norman Mailer: *An American Dream*
John Berryman: *77 Dream Songs*

Political/Social

Martin Luther King heads 4,000 Civil Rights demonstrators from Selma to Montgomery, Alabama.
Racial violence over voter registration in Selma.
Assassination of Malcolm X in New York.
Lyndon Baines Johnson inaugurated as 36th President.
Severe race riots in Watts.
Large-scale bombings of North Viet Nam.
Ralph Nader: *Unsafe at Any Speed.*
Bob Dylan "goes electric" at the Newport Jazz Festival.
Herbert Marcuse: *Culture and Society*
Popular songs include: *Like a Rolling Stone, Mr. Tambourine Man, King of the Road, It Was a Very Good Year, Downtown, I Can't Get No Satisfaction.*

1966

Film

Independent
Ed Emshwiller: *Relativity*
Bruce Baillie: *Castro Street*
Tony Conrad: *The Flicker*
George Landow: *Film in Which There Appear Sprocket Holes, Edge Lettering, Dirt Particles, Etc.*
Jonas Mekas: *Notes on the Circus* and *Report from Millbrook*
Paul Sharits: *Ray Gun Virus* and *Word Movie-Fluxfilm*
Andy Warhol: *Chelsea Girls*
Robert Downey: *Chafed Elbows*
Peter Kubelka: *Unsere Afrikareise*
D.A. Pennebaker: *Don't Look Back*
Founding of Millennium Film Workshop in New York.
Film Culture 43 devotes special issue to "Expanded Arts" recognizing increased activity in intermedia events.

Foreign
Jean-Luc Godard: *2 or 3 Things I Know About Her* and *Masculin-Feminin*
Karel Reisz: *Morgan!*
Michelangelo Antonioni: *Blow-up*

Hollywood
Mike Nichols: *Who's Afraid of Virginia Woolf?*

The Arts

Visual Art
New York exhibitions of *Primary Structures* at the Jewish Museum, *Systematic Painting* at the Guggenheim, and *10X10* at Dwan represent emerging "minimal," "serial," and "conceptual" art movements. Artists include Carl Andre, Dan Flavin, Robert Morris and Robert Smithson among others.

Literature
Louis Zukofsky: *All: The Collected Shorter Poems 1958–64*
Truman Capote: *In Cold Blood*

Dance
Yvonne Rainer: *The Mind is a Muscle*

Political/Social

First demonstration against Viet Nam war leads to International Days of Protest against U.S. policy and campaign to encourage desertion.
Race riots in Chicago, Brooklyn and Cleveland.
Black Panthers organize in Oakland and the Black Power movement emerges under the leadership of Stokely Carmichael.
Foundation of the National Organization of Women (NOW) by Betty Friedan.
Emergence of the Hippy movement.
Timothy Leary advocates the use of LSD.
Quotations of Chairman Mao is published.
Color TV becomes popular.
Popular songs include: *The Sounds of Silence, We Can Work It Out, These Boots are Made for Walking, Good Lovin', Paint It Black, Paperback Writer, Strangers in the Night, Wild Thing, Summer in the City, Ballad of the Green Berets, Reach Out I'll Be There, You Keep Me Hangin' On, Good Vibrations.*

1967

Film

Independent
George Landow: *Diploteratology or Bardo Follies*
Gregory Markopoulos: *The Illiac Passion*
Michael Snow: *Wavelength*
Andy Warhol: *I, a Man, Bike Boy, Lonesome Cowboys*
Jim McBride: *David Holzman's Diary*
Frederick Wiseman: *Titicut Follies*
Paul Sharits: *Piece Mandala/End War*
Shirley Clarke: *Portrait of Jason*
Fourth Experimental Film Competition at Knokke-le-Zoute awards *Wavelength* and Steve Dwoskin.
Publications include Gregory Battcock, ed.: *New American Cinema: A Critical Anthology,* and Sheldon Renan: *The Underground Film.*

Foreign
Luis Buñuel: *Belle de Jour*
Roberto Rossellini: *The Rise and Fall of Louis XIV*
Joseph Losey: *Accident*

Hollywood
Arthur Penn: *Bonnie and Clyde*
Stanley Kramer: *Guess Who's Coming to Dinner*
Mike Nichols: *The Graduate*

The Arts

Literature
Michael McClure: *The Beard* (play)

Music
Steve Reich composes *Piano Phase/Violin Phase*
John Cage publishes *A Year From Monday* (collected writings) and organizes the first "Musicircus," simultaneous performances of as much unrelated music as possible.

Political/Social

Peace marches in New York, Washington and San Francisco.
Race riots in Newark and Detroit.
Arab/Israeli Six Day War.
Che Guevara killed by Bolivian troops.
Twiggy, British fashion model, becomes trend setter.
Monterey Pop Festival features Janis Joplin, Jimi Hendrix and Otis Redding among others.
The Rolling Stones appear on the Ed Sullivan Show.
Popular songs include: *Ruby Tuesday, Penny Lane, Let's Spend the Night Together, Light My Fire, Love is Here and Now You're Gone, Happy Together, Groovin', All You Need is Love, Ode to Billy Joe, Respect.*

Filmography

John Cassavetes

1959   *Shadows*
1961   *Too Late Blues*
1962   *A Child Is Waiting*
1968   *Faces*
1970   *Husbands*
1971   *Minnie and Moskowitz*
1974   *A Woman Under the Influence*
1976   *The Killing of a Chinese Bookie*
1978   *Opening Night*
1980   *Gloria*

Shirley Clarke

1953   *Dance in the Sun*
1954   *In Paris Parks*
1955   *Bullfight*
1957   *A Moment in Love*
1958   *Brussels "Loops"*
1958-59   *Bridges-Go-Round*
1959   *Skyscraper*
1960   *A Scary Time*
1960   *The Connection*
1963   *The Cool World*
1964   *A Love Letter to the World*
1967   *Portrait of Jason*
1980   *Four Journeys into Mystic Time*
     consists of:
     Mysterium
     Trans (video and film)
     One-Two-Three (video)
     Initiation
1981   *Savage/Love* (video)
1982   *Tongues* (video)

Robert Downey

1963   *Balls Bluff*
1964   *Babo 73*
1966   *Chafed Elbows*
1967   *Sweet Smell of Sex*
1968   *No More Excuses*
1969   *Putney Swope*
1970   *Pound*
1972   *Greaser's Palace*
1973   *Sticks and Bones* (television)
1979   *Jive*
1980   *Up the Academy*
1983   *Moonbeam*

Robert Frank

1959   *Pull My Daisy* (with Alfred Leslie)
1961   *The Sins of Jesus*
1963   *OK and Here*
1964   *Me and My Brother*
1965   *Hungerstrike*
1968   *Conversations in Vermont*
1971   *About me a musical*
1972   *Cocksucker Blues*
1975   *Keep Busy*
1980   *Life Dances On*
1981   *Energy and How To Get It*

George Kuchar

1954   *The Wet Destruction of the Atlantic Empire*
     (8mm, with Mike Kuchar)
1957   *Screwball* (8mm, with Mike Kuchar)
     The Naked and the Nude
     (8mm, with Mike Kuchar)
1958   *The Slasher* (8mm, with Mike Kuchar)
1959   *A Tub Named Desire*
     (8mm, with Mike Kuchar)
     The Thief and the Stripper
     (8mm, with Mike Kuchar)
1960   *I Was a Teenage Rumpot*
     (8mm, with Mike Kuchar)
1961   *Pussy on a Hot Tin Roof*
     (8mm, with Mike Kuchar)
     Night of the Bomb
     (8mm, with Mike Kuchar)
1962   *A Woman Distressed* (8mm)
     Sylvia's Promise (8mm, with Mike Kuchar)
1963   *A Town Called Tempest* (8mm)
     Confessions of Babette
     (8mm, with Mike Kuchar)
     Lust for Ecstasy (8mm)
     Anita Needs Me (8mm)
     Tootsies in Autumn (8mm)
1964   *The Lovers of Eternity* (8mm)
1965   *Corruption of the Damned*
1966   *Hold Me While I'm Naked*
     Leisure
     Mosholu Holiday
1967   *Eclipse of the Sun Virgin*
     Color Me Shameless
     The Lady from Sands Point
1968   *Knockturne*
     Unstrap Me
     House of the White People
     Encyclopedia of the Blessed
1969   *The Mammal Palace*
1970   *Pagan Rhapsody*
1971   *Portrait of Ramona*
1973   *The Sunshine Sisters*
     The Devil's Cleavage
1976   *A Reason to Live*
     Back to Nature
1977   *I, An Actress*
     KY Kapers
     Wild Night in El Reno
1978   *Forever and Always*
     The Mongreloid
1979   *Blips*
1980   *Aqueerius*
     The Nocturnal Immaculation
1981   *Yolanda*
     The Woman and the Dress

Alfred Leslie

1959   *Pull My Daisy* (with Robert Frank)
1964   *The Last Clean Shirt*
1966   *Philosophy in the Bedroom*

Ben Maddow

1937	*China Strikes Back* (with Irving Lerner, Jay Leyda, Sidney Meyers)
1939-40	*The White Flood* (with Lionel Berman, Sidney Meyers)
1941	*The History and Romance of Transportation* (with Lionel Berman, Sidney Meyers)
1944	*The Bridge* (with Willard Van Dyke)
1951	*The Steps of Age*
1959	*The Savage Eye* (with Ben Maddow and Joseph Strick)
1963	*An Affair of the Skin*
1969	*Storm of Strangers*

Jim McBride

1967	*David Holzman's Diary*
1969	*My Girlfriend's Wedding*
1972	*Glen and Randa*
1974	*Hot Times*
1983	*Breathless*

Adolfas Mekas

1953	*Silent Journey* (with Jonas Mekas)
1963	*Hallelujah the Hills*
1965	*The Double-Barreled Detective Story* *Skyscraper*
1967	*Windflowers*
1968	*Sweet Victory* (television commercials)
1970	*Compañeras and Compañeros* (with Barbara and David Stone)
1972	*Going Home* (with Pola Chapelle)
1982	*Zamzok*

Jonas Mekas

1953	*Silent Journey* (with Adolfas Mekas)
1961	*Guns of the Trees*
1963	*Film Magazine of the Arts*
1964	*The Brig* *Award Presentation to Andy Warhol*
1966	*Report from Millbrook* *Cassis* *Notes on the Circus*
1968	*Time & Fortune Viet Nam Newsreel* *Diaries, Notes & Sketches*
1971	*Reminiscences of a Journey to Lithuania*
1976	*Lost, Lost, Lost*
1978	*In Between* *Notes for Jerome*
1979-80	*Paradise Not Yet Lost* *(Oona's Third Year)*

Sidney Meyers

1937	*China Strikes Back* (with Jay Ledya, Ben Maddow, Irving Lerner)
1938	*People of the Cumberland* (with Ralph Steiner, Elia Kazan)
1939-40	*The White Flood* (with Lionel Berman, Ben Maddow)
1941	*The History and Romance of Transportation* (with Lionel Berman, Ben Maddow)
1948	*The Quiet One*
1959	*The Savage Eye* (with Ben Maddow, Joseph Strick)

Ron Rice

1960	*The Flower Thief*
1962	*Senseless*
1963	*The Queen of Sheba Meets The Atom Man*
1964	*Chumlum*

Michael Roemer

1949	*A Touch of the Times* (with Robert Young)
1960	*Parlons Francais* (television series)
1962	*The Inferno* (NBC television *White Paper* series, with Robert Young)
1964	*Nothing But a Man* (with Robert Young)
1976	*Dying* (television)
1980	*Pilgrim, Farewell* (television)
1983	*Haunted* (television)

Lionel Rogosin

1956	*On the Bowery*
1959	*Come Back, Africa*
1963	*Oysters Are In Season*
1964	*Arab-Israeli Dialogue*
1965	*Good Times, Wonderful Times*
1966	*How Do You Like Them Bananas*
1970	*Black Roots*
1972	*Black Fantasy*
1973	*Woodcutters of the Deep South*

Joseph Strick

1948	*Muscle Beach* (with Irving Lerner)
1953	*The Big Break*
1959	*The Savage Eye* (with Sidney Meyers, Ben Maddow)
1963	*The Balcony*
1967	*Ulysses*
1968	*Justine* (with George Cukor)
1970	*Tropic of Cancer* *Interviews with MyLai Veterans*
1973	*Road Movie*
1977	*Portrait of the Artist as a Young Man*

Robert Young

1949	*A Touch of the Times* (with Michael Roemer)
1949-55	*Rules and Laws: It Takes Everybody to Build This Land* *Witch Doctor* *Wonders of the Sea* (television) *Secrets of the Reef*
1956	*Life of the Molds* (with Charles Pfizer)
1957-58	*India* (television *High Adventure* program)
1958-59	*Horizons of Science* (five education films)
1959	*Danger Island* (television *High Adventure* program)
1960	*Sit-In* (NBC television *White Paper* series) *Wide World* (NBC television series)
1961	*Angola: Journey to a War* (NBC television *White Paper* series) *Anatomy of a Hospital* (NBC television *White Paper* series)
1962	*The Inferno* (NBC television *White Paper* series, with Michael Roemer) *Cortile Cascino* (NBC television *White Paper* series; never shown)
1964	*Nothing But A Man* (with Michael Roemer)
1966	*In the World of Sharks* (with Peter Gimbel)
1971	*The Eskimo: Fight for Life* (television)
1973	*Children of the Fields* (television)
1976	*Search for the Great Apes* (television) *Alambrista* (television)
1977	*Short Eyes*
1978	*Rich Kids*
1980	*One Trick Pony*
1982	*The Ballad of Gregorio Cortez* (television)

Bibliography

This bibliography, primarily confined to English-language material, lists general sources both on the cultural background of the films in the series and on the individual films and filmmakers. In the individual film listings, periodicals are listed first, followed by books containing information on the specific title.

Bill Horrigan

Books Related to the Historical and Cultural Period

Against Interpretation, Susan Sontag, NY: Farrar, Strauss, 1966
The Age of Paranoia: How the Sixties Ended, Rolling Stone, NY: Pocket Books, 1972
The Armies of the Night, Norman Mailer, NY: New American Library, 1968
The Beat Generation, Bruce Cook, NY: Scribners, 1971
Coming Apart: An Informal History of America in the 1960s, William L. O'Neill, Chicago: Quadrangle Books, 1971
Gates of Eden: American Culture in the Sixties, Morris Dickstein, NY: Basic Books, Inc., 1977
Moving Through Here, Don McNeill, NY: Knopf, 1970
The New Journalism, ed. Tom Wolfe and E.W. Johnson, NY: Harper & Row, 1973
The Performing Self, Richard Poirier, NY: Oxford University Press, 1971
Popism: The Warhol 60s, Andy Warhol and Pat Hacker, NY: Harcourt Brace Jovanovich, 1980
The Scene: Reports on Post-Modern Art, Calvin Tomkins, NY: Viking Press, 1976
The Sixties, ed. Lynda Rosen Obst, NY: Random House/Rolling Stone Press, 1977

Books and Catalogues Related to Films in the Series

American Independents: A Festival of American Independent Feature Films, presented by the Film Fund and the Film Society of Lincoln Center (essays by Sandra Schulberg and Miles Mogulescu), 1979
The American Experimental Film in the Last Decade, Colin Young, Paris: UNESCO Publication, 12 October 1964
The Beat, the Square and the Hip: The New American Cinema and Its Cultural Milieu, Blaine Allen, Ph.D. dissertation, Northwestern University, 1983
The Documentary Tradition from "Nanook" to "Woodstock," ed. Lewis Jacobs, NY: Hopkinson and Blake, 1971
Festival of Two Worlds: The New American Cinema, ed. David C. Stone, Spoleto, Italy, 1961
Film Culture Reader, ed. and introduced P. Adams Sitney, NY: Praeger Publishers, 1970
An Introduction to the American Underground Film, Sheldon Renan, NY: E.P. Dutton & Co., 1967
Jeune Cinéma Américain, Paul and Jean-Louis Leutrat, Premier Plan 46, 1967
Living Cinema, Louis Marcorelles, NY: Praeger Publishers, 1973
Movie Journal: The Rise of a New American Cinema, Jonas Mekas, NY: Collier Books, 1972
The New American Cinema: A Critical Anthology, ed. Gregory Battcock, NY: E.P. Dutton & Co., 1967
On Movies, Dwight Macdonald, Englewood Cliffs, NJ: Prentice-Hall, 1969
Underground Film: A Critical History, Parker Tyler, NY: Grove Press, 1969

Articles Related to Films in the Series

American Film, March 1982, "The Short Happy Life of the Charles," J. Hoberman, pp 22, 34
Cinemaction, n 12, 1980, "Avant-Garde and Political Film in the United States," B. Ruby Rich and Chuck Kleinhans
Esquire, May 1962, "La Nouvelle Vague de New York," Walter Ross, pp 35–47
Film Comment, v 2, n 3, Summer 1964, "Survey Among Unsuccessful Applicants for the Ford Foundation Film Grants," ed. Gordon Hitchens
Film Culture, n 19, 1959, "A Call for a New Generation of Film Makers," Jonas Mekas (also in *Film Culture Reader,* pp 73-75)
Film Culture, n 21, Summer 1960, "Cinema of the New Generation," Jonas Mekas, pp 1–20
Film Culture, n 24, Summer 1962, "Notes on the New American Cinema," Jonas Mekas, pp 6–16 (also in *Film Culture Reader,* pp 87–107)
Film Culture, n 24, Summer 1962, "Glossary of the New American Cinema," unsigned, pp 21–22
Film Culture, n 24, Summer 1962, "Once More on the New Generation," Alexander Karagarov, pp 22– 23
Film Culture, n 22/23, Summer 1961, "The First Statement of the New American Cinema Group," pp 131–133 (also in *Film Culture Reader,* pp 79–83)
Film Culture, n 22/23, Summer 1961, "Film Unions and the Low-Budget Independent Film Production—An Exploratory Discussion," pp 134–150
Film Reader, n 5, 1982, "The Beat, the Hip and the Square," Blaine Allen, pp 257–269
Film Quarterly, v 13, n 4, Spring 1960, "The Expensive Art—A Discussion of Film Distribution and Exhibition in the United States," pp 19–34
Film Quarterly, v 14, n 3, Spring 1961, "New Wave—or Gesture?," Colin Young and Gideon Bachman
Sight and Sound, Winter 1960/61, "Independents in New York," Cecile Starr, pp 22–23
Sight and Sound, Spring 1962, "New York Letter," Arlene Croce
Vision: A Journal of Film Comment, v 1, n 2, Summer 1962, "Back to the Greeks," Harry Feldman, pp 13–15
Vision: A Journal of Film Comment, v 1, n 2, Summer 1962, "Towards an Abstract Cinema? Not Yet," John Craddock, pp 21–23

The Savage Eye
Ben Maddow, Sidney Meyers, Joseph Strick

Film Culture, n 22–23, 1961, "The Modern Hero: The Nongenue," A.J. Alexander, pp 81–90
Film Quarterly, v 13, n 4, 1960, *The Savage Eye,* Benjamin T. Jackson, pp 58–59
Films and Filming, v 6, n 4, Jan. 1960, Paul Rotha, pp 21, 26
The New York Times, June 7, 1960, A.H. Weiler
The New Yorker, June 18, 1960, pp 108–110
Sight and Sound, Winter 1959/60, *The Savage Eye,* Eric Rhode, p 37

The Documentary Tradition from "Nanook" to "Woodstock," ed. Lewis Jacobs, *The Savage Eye,* Archer Winsten, pp 341–342
On Movies, Dwight Macdonald, pp 320—322

Shadows
John Cassavetes

L'Avant-Scène, n 197, Dec. 1977, ed. Raymond Lefèbre (script)
Film Comment, v 1, n 4, 1963, "An Interview with Hugh Hurd," Clara Hoover, pp 24–27
Film Culture, n 24, Spring 1962, "For *Shadows,* Against *Pull My Daisy,*" Parker Tyler, pp 28–33, (also in *Film Culture Reader,* pp 108–117)
Film Quarterly, v 13, n 3, Spring 1960, *Shadows,* Albert Johnson, pp 32–34
Film Quarterly, v 14, n 3, Spring 1961, "New Wave—or Gesture?," Colin Young and Gideon Bachman
Films and Filming, v 7, n 2, Nov. 1960, Raymond Durgnat, pp 29–30
Films and Filming, v 7, n 5, Feb. 1961, ". . . and the Pursuit of Happiness," John Cassavetes, pp 7–8
New Republic, March 6, 1961, pp 20–21
The New York Times, March 22, 1961, Bosley Crowther
The New Yorker, April 1, 1961, pp 122–125
Newsweek, April 3, 1961, p 92
Playboy, May 1961, p 22
Saturday Review, April 1, 1961, p 26
Sight and Sound, Autumn 1960, "Cassavetes in London," John Russell Taylor, pp 177–178
Sight and Sound, Autumn 1960, *Shadows,* Derek Prouse, pp 192–193
Sight and Sound, Autumn 1962, "How Art Is True," Tom Milne, pp 166–171
Time, March 24, 1961, p 72

From Sambo to Superspade, Daniel J. Leab, Boston: Houghton Mifflin Company, 1975, pp 214–215
Hollywood Renaissance, Diane Jacobs, NY: Delta Books, 1980, pp 27–54
Movie Journal, Jonas Mekas, pp 10–11
On Movies, Dwight Macdonald, pp 311–312
Toms, Coons, Mulattoes, Mammies and Bucks, Donald Bogle, NY: Viking Press, 1973, p 200
Underground Film, Parker Tyler, pp 201–203

Pull My Daisy
Robert Frank and Alfred Leslie

Cinema Dope, n 17, April 1979, Robert Frank bio-filmography, D.J. Badder, p 38
Afterimage, Summer 1980, "'The Americas' and *The Americans,*" John Brumfield, pp 8–15
Film Culture, n 24, Spring 1962, "For *Shadows,* Against *Pull My Daisy,*" Parker Tyler, pp 28–33
Monthly Film Bulletin, Jan. 1974, *Pull My Daisy,* Tony Rayns, p 17
New Republic, May 16, 1960, pp 22–23
Time, Dec. 14, 1959, p 66

The Beat Generation, Bruce Cook, NY: Scribners, 1971
Desolate Angel: Jack Kerouac and the Beat Generation and America, Dennis McNally, NY: Random House, pp 262–264
The Gutman Letter, Walter Gutman, NY: Something Else Press, 1969, pp 29–33
Jack's Book, Barry Gifford, NY: St. Martin's Press, 1978, pp 257–262
Kerouac: A Biography, Ann Charters, NY: Warner Books, 1974, p 3
Movie Journal, Jonas Mekas, pp 5–6
Naked Angels, John Tytell, NY: McGraw-Hill, 1976, pp 28–29
On Movies, Dwight Macdonald, pp 310–311
The Real Bohemia: A Sociological and Psychological Study of the "Beats," Francis J. Rigney and L. Douglas Smith, NY: Basic Books, 1961

The Queen of Sheba Meets The Atom Man
Ron Rice

Film Comment, v 1, n 3, 1962, "Ron Rice and His Work," Mary Batten, pp 30–31
Film Comment, v 2, n 3, Summer 1964, "Survey Among Unsuccessful Applicants for the Ford Foundation Film Grants," ed. Gordon Hitchens, p 29
Film Culture, n 25, Summer 1962, "*The Sin of Jesus* and *The Flower Thief,*" P. Adams Sitney, pp 30–32
Film Culture, n 25, Summer 1962, "A Statement," Ron Rice, p 71
Film Culture, n 39, Winter 1965, "Ron Rice: Diaries, Notebooks, Documents," Ron Rice, pp 87–125
Film Culture, n 48–49, Winter/Spring 1970, "Two Films by Ron Rice," Fred Camper, pp 30–31

Film-Makers' Cooperative Catalogue, n 6, 1975, pp 207–208
An Introduction to the American Underground Film, Sheldon Renan, pp 175–178
Movie Journal, Jonas Mekas, pp 63–64; 64–65; 121–122; 170–172
The New American Cinema: A Critical Anthology, ed. Gregory Battcock, pp 47–48
Underground Film: A Critical History, Parker Tyler, p 48

Nothing But A Man
Michael Roemer and Robert Young

American Film, July/August 1982, "Robert M. Young's Ordinary People," Gerald Peary, pp 66–71
Ebony, April 1965, pp 198–201
Film Comment, v 2, n 4, 1965, "The Second New York Film Festival," Andrew Sarris, pp 12–16
Film Comment, v 3, n 1, Winter 1965, "*Nothing But a Man,*" William Howton
Film Comment, v 3, n 2, Spring 1966, "Michael Roemer and Robert Young," Saul B. Cohen, pp 8– 14
Film Heritage, v 3, n 2, Winter 1967/68, "Conversation with Michael Roemer," Anne Widmark, pp 29–33
Life, Feb. 19, 1965, p 15
New Republic, Jan 16, 1965, pp 67–68
The New York Times, April 21, 1964, Bosley Crowther
The New Yorker, Jan. 9, 1965, p 104
Newsweek, Jan. 11, 1965, p 79
Playboy, March 1965, p 34
Positif, n 75, May 1966, "Le Jeune Cinema Americain," Roger Tailleur, pp 120–122
The Reporter, Oct. 26, 1961, "New Wave and The Old Rock," Michael Roemer, pp 45–46
Saturday Review, Jan. 30, 1965, p 40
Sight and Sound, Autumn 1964, "Festivals 64: Venice," Tom Milne, p 186
Time, Jan. 15, 1965, p 89

From Sambo to Superspade, Daniel J. Leab, pp 199–200
Movie Journal, Jonas Mekas, pp 199–201

The Cool World
Shirley Clarke

Ebony, July 1965, pp 43–44
Film Comment, v 2, n 2, 1964, "Shirley Clarke at Venice: An Interview with Harriet Polt," pp 31–32
Film Comment, v 2, n 2, 1964, "*The Cool World,*" Jesse Walker, pp 51–52
Film Comment, v 2, n 2, 1964, "*The Cool World,*" Gordon Hitchens, pp 52–53
Film Culture, n 44, Spring 1967, "Interview with Shirley Clarke," Gretchen Berg, pp 52–55
Film Culture, n 27, 1962/63, "Shirley Clarke Shooting *The Cool World,*" photographs by Leroy McLucas, p 37
Film Culture, n 46, Autumn 67, "A Conversation—Shirley Clarke and Storm de Hirsch," pp 44–54
Film Quarterly, v 13, n 4, Summer 1960, "The Films of Shirley Clarke," Henry Breitrose, pp 57–58
Film Quarterly, v 17, n 2, Winter 1963/64, "*The Cool World,*" Harriet Polt, pp 63–64
Films and Filming, v 10, n 3, Dec. 1963, "*The Cool World,*" Shirley Clarke, pp 7–8
Life, April 24, 1964, p 15
New Republic, May 23, 1964, p 124
The New York Times, April 21, 1964, Bosley Crowther
The New Yorker, April 25, 1964, pp 171–172
Newsweek, April 20, 1964, p 114
Take One, v 3, n 2, Nov/Dec 1970, "Shirley Clarke: Image and Images," Susan Rice, pp 20–22
Time, April 17, 1964, p 123
The Village Voice, April 23, 1964, Andrew Sarris, p 16

On Movies, Dwight Macdonald, pp 323–327

Babo 73
Robert Downey

Film Reader, n 1, 1975, p 120
The New Yorker, Oct. 17, 1964, p 187

Movie Journal, Jonas Mekas, pp 159–160

Hold Me While I'm Naked
George Kuchar

Canyon Cinema News, n 1, Jan/Feb 1974,
"Reflections," George Kuchar, pp 8–9
Film Culture, n 33, 1964, "George Kuchar Speaks
on Films and Truth"
Film Culture, n 45, Summer 1967, "Interview with
the Kuchar Brothers," Sheldon Renan, pp 47–51
Monthly Film Bulletin, Nov. 1978, "A Kuchar
Quickie," Tony Rayns, p 234; "Checklist 114—
George Kuchar and Mike Kuchar," T. Mayer,
pp 231–232
The Village Voice, Sept. 1966, *"Hold Me While I'm
Naked,"* James Stoller, p 20
The Village Voice, Dec. 8, 1975, "How the Kuchar
Brothers Found Hollywood in the Bronx,"
J. Hoberman, p 18

Film-Makers' Cooperative Catalogue, n 6, 1975,
pp 146–149
An Introduction to the American Underground Film,
Sheldon Renan, pp 157–161
Movie Journal, Jonas Mekas, pp 122–126

Hallelujah the Hills
Adolfas Mekas

L'Avant-Scène, n 64, Nov. 1966 (script)
Cahiers du Cinéma, n 145, July 1963, *"Hallelujah
the Hills,"* B.S.
Film Quarterly, v 17, n 1, Fall 1963, *"Hallelujah the
Hills,"* Harriet Polt, pp 48–49
Films and Filming, v 10, n 5, Feb. 1964, *"Hallelujah
the Hills,"* Raymond Durgnat, p 34
Hollywood Reporter, Feb. 21, 1964, James Powers
Manchester Guardian, Jan 2, 1964, Richard Roud
The New Yorker, Dec. 21, 1963
The New York Times, Dec. 17, 1963, Eugene
Archer
Saturday Review, Feb. 29, 1964
Time, Dec. 13, 1963
Variety, May 15, 1963, Gene Moskowitz
The Village Voice, Dec. 19, 1963, Herman
Weinberg

Film-Makers' Cooperative Catalogue, n 6, 1975,
p 176
The New American Cinema, ed. Gregory Battcock,
pp 202–204
On Movies, Dwight Macdonald, pp 327–330
Underground Film, Parker Tyler, pp 47–48

Come Back, Africa
Lionel Rogosin

Film Comment, v 2, n 4, 1964, "Odyssey from
Hollywood to New York," Carl Lerner, pp 2–11
Film Culture, n 21, Summer 1960, "Interpreting
Reality (Notes on the Esthetics and Practices of
Improvisational Acting)," Lionel Rogosin, pp 20–28
Film Culture, n 24, Spring 1962, "Rogosin and
Documentary," Peter Davis, pp 25–28
Film Quarterly, v 13, n 4, Summer 1960, *"Come
Back, Africa,"* Cecile Starr and Roger Sandell,
pp 58–59
Films and Filming, v 6, n 4, Jan. 1960, Paul Rotha,
pp 21, 26
New Republic, May 16, 1960, p 22
The New York Times, April 5, 1960, Bosley
Crowther
The New Yorker, April 16, 1960, p 149
Saturday Review, April 2, 1960, p 26
Sight and Sound, Winter 1959/60, "London
Festival," Derek Hill, p 9
Sight and Sound, Summer 1960, "New York Letter,"
Cecile Starr, pp 140–141

*The Documentary Tradition from "Nanook" to
"Woodstock,"* ed. Lewis Jacobs, *Come Back, Africa,*
Archer Winsten, pp 339–340
Movie Journal, Jonas Mekas, pp 13–15

The Brig
Jonas Mekas

Film-Makers' Cooperative Catalogue, n 6, 1975,
pp 177–179
Literature/Film Quarterly, v 1, n 2, April 1973,
"Jonas Mekas Interviewed," Gerald Barrett,
pp 103–112
The New York Times, Sept. 21, 1964, Howard
Thompson
The New Yorker, April 23, 1966, pp 131–132
The New Yorker, Jan. 6, 1973, "Profiles: All Pockets
Open," Calvin Tompkins, pp 31–49
Newsweek, April 25, 1966, p 90
Sight and Sound, Autumn 1964, "Festivals 64:
Venice," Tom Milne, p 186
Tulane Drama Review, v 8, n 3, Spring 1964, *"The
Brig,"* (script), Kenneth H. Brown
The Village Voice, April 21, 1966, p 29

An Introduction to the American Underground Film,
Sheldon Renan, pp 167–169
Movie Journal, Jonas Mekas, pp 190–194; 247–250

David Holzman's Diary
Jim McBride

Cinema, v 5, n 1, 1969, "More Notes from the
Underground," L.M. Kit Carson
Ecran, n 34, March 1975, *"Le journal intime de David
Holzman,"* M. Martin, pp 77–78
Film Library Quarterly, Summer 1969, *"David
Holzman's Diary,"* L.M. Kit Carson, pp 20–22
Film Quarterly, v 23, n 4, Summer 1970, *"David
Holzman's Diary,"* Sidney Hollister, pp 50–52
Filmmakers' Newsletter, Aug. 75, "Films on
Filmmaking," A. Reilly, pp 34–35
Film Reader, n 1, 1975, p 131
Image et Son, n 296, May 1975, *"Le journal intime
de David Holzman,"* A. Garel, pp 94–97
Jeune Cinéma, n 85, March 1975, "Jim McBride:
limites du cinéma verité," Jean Delmas, pp 19–24
The New York Times, Dec. 9, 1973, Vincent Canby
Positif, n 158, April 1974, "Recontre avec Jim
McBride," Jonathan Rosenbaum, pp 37–40
Positif, n 166, Feb. 1975, "Narcisse au miroir ou
l'hygiène du cinéma," O. Eyquem, pp 55–57
Velvet Light Trap, n 13, 1974, "Let It Run," P. Hogue,
pp 40–44

David Holzman's Diary, L.M. Kit Carson, NY: Farrar,
Strauss, Giroux, 1970

Portrait of Jason
Shirley Clarke

Cinema, v 4, n 1, Spring 1968, *"Portrait of Jason,"*
Quentin Guerlain, p 48
Commonweal, Oct. 27, 1967, p 120
Film Quarterly, v 22, n 1, Fall 1968, *"Portrait of
Jason,"* Ernest Callenbach, pp 74–77
Film Culture, n 44, Spring 1967, "Interview with
Shirley Clarke," Gretchen Berg, pp 52–55
Monthly Film Bulletin, March 1978, *"Portrait of
Jason,"* Verina Glaessner, p 51
The Nation, Oct. 30, 1967, pp 445–446
The New York Times, Sept. 30, 1967, Vincent
Canby
The New Yorker, Oct. 14, 1967, p 159
Sight and Sound, Winter 1967/68, "London Film
Festival," James Price, p 10
Take One, v 1, n 7, 1967, *"Portrait of Jason,"* Jack
Hofsess, pp 24–26
The Village Voice, Oct. 5, 1967, *"Portrait of Jason,"*
James Stoller, p 33

Film 67/68, ed. Richard Schickel and John Simon,
NY: Simon and Schuster, 1968: "Desparate,"
Joseph Morgenstern, pp 253–255
Movie Journal, Jonas Mekas, pp 289–291
Screening the Sexes, Parker Tyler, Garden City, NY:
Anchor Books, 1973, p 153
Toms, Coons, Mulattoes, Mammies and Bucks,
Donald Bogle, p 201

Film Credits

Program I

The Savage Eye
(1959)   67 minutes

A film by Ben Maddow, Sidney Meyers and Joseph Strick
Cinematography: Haskell Wexler, Jack Couffer and Helen Levitt
Additional photography: Sy Wexler and Joel Coleman
Sound: Leroy Robbins
Sound editor: Verna Fields
Music composed and conducted by Leonard Rosenmann
With: Barbara Baxley as Judith McGuire, Gary Merrill as the Poet, Herschel Bernardi as Kirtz, Jean Hidey as Venus the Body, Elizabeth Zemach as the Nurse

Shadows
(1959)   82 minutes

Director: John Cassavetes
Producer: Maurice McEndree
Associate producer: Seymour Cassel
Cinematography: Erich Kollmar
Editor: Maurice McEndree
Supervising film editor: Len Appelson
Sound: Jay Crecco
Saxophone solos: Shafi Hadi
Additional music: Charles Mingus
With: Ben Carruthers, Lelia Goldoni, Hugh Hurd, Anthony Ray, Dennis Sallas, Tom Allen, David Pokitillow, Rupert Crosse, Davey Jones, Pir Marini, Victoria Vargas, Jack Ackerman, Jacqueline Walcott, Cliff Carnell, Jay Crecco, Ronald Maccone, Bob Reeh, Joyce Miles, Nancy Deale, Gigi Brooks, Lynn Hamelton, Marilyn Clark, Joanne Sages, Jed McGarvey, Greta Thysen

Program II

Pull My Daisy
(1959)   29 minutes

Adapted, photographed and directed by Robert Frank and Alfred Leslie
Writer and narrator: Jack Kerouac
Editors: Leon Prochnik, Robert Frank and Alfred Leslie
Music composed and conducted by David Amram
Lyrics by Allen Ginsberg and Jack Kerouac
"The Crazy Daisy" sung by Anita Ellis
With: Mooney Pebbles as Bishop, Allen Ginsberg as Allen, Gregory Corso as Gregory, Peter Orlovsky as Peter, Larry Rivers as Milo, Beltiane (Delphine Seyrig) as Milo's wife, David Amram as Mez McGillicuddy, Alice Neel as Bishop's mother, Sally Gross as Bishop's sister, Denise Parker as the girl in bed, Pablo Frank as the little boy

The Queen of Sheba Meets The Atom Man
(1963)   110 minutes

A film by Ron Rice
With: Winifred Bryan, Taylor Mead, Jack Smith

Program III

Nothing But A Man
(1964)   92 minutes

Director: Michael Roemer
Producers: Robert Young, Michael Roemer and Robert Rubin in association with Du Art Film Laboratories
Writers: Michael Roemer and Robert Young
Cinematography: Robert Young
Editor: Luke Bennett
Sound: Robert Rubin
With: Ivan Dixon as Duff Anderson, Abbey Lincoln as Josie, Julius Harris as Will Anderson, Gloria Foster as Lee, Martin Priest as Driver, Leonard Parker as Frankie, Yaphet Kotto as Jocko, Stanley Greene as Rev. Mr. Dawson

The Cool World
(1963)   104 minutes

Director: Shirley Clarke
Producer: Frederick Wiseman
Screenplay by Shirley Clarke and Carl Lee from the novel by Warren Miller and the play by Warren Miller and Robert Rossen
Cinematography: Baird Bryant
Editor: Shirley Clarke
Music composed and arranged by Mal Waldron
Casting and dialogue director: Carl Lee
With: Hampton Clanton as Duke, Carl Lee as Priest, Yolanda Rodríguez as LuAnne, Clarence Williams as Blood, Gary Bolling as Littleman, Bostic Felton as Rod, Gloria Foster as Mrs. Custis, John Marriott as Hurst, Georgia Burke as Grandma, Marilyn Cox as Miss Dewpoint, Jerome Raphael as Mr. Shapiro, Mel Stewart as the con-man, Joseph Dennis as Douglas Thuston, Joe Oliver as Angel, Charles Richardson as Beep Bop, Bruce Edwards as Warrior

Program IV

Babo 73
(1964)   57 minutes

Written, produced and directed by Robert Downey
Cinematography: William Waering
Editor: Fred Von Bernewitz
Sound: John Fodor
Music: Ton O'Horgan assisted by Nicky Zann 'n' the Vitamins
With: James Antonio, Tom Gaines, James Greene, Taylor Mead as The President, Richard Roat, William Rydell

Hold Me While I'm Naked
(1966)   15 minutes

A film by George Kuchar
With: Donna Kerness, Hope Morris, Steve Packard, Andrea Lunin
Miss Kerness' clothes by Hope Morris

Hallelujah the Hills
(1963)   82 minutes

Written and directed by Adolfas Mekas
Assistant director: Jonas Mekas
Producer: David C. Stone

Cinematography: Ed Emshwiller
Editor: Adolfas Mekas
Assistant editor: Louis Brigante
Script girl: Barbara Stone
Spiritual advisor: H.G.W.
Costumes and Props: Bathsheba
Equipment: Florman and Babbs, Inc.
Music composed and conducted by Meyer Kupferman
With: Peter H. Beard as Jack, Sheila Finn as Jack's Vera, Martin Greenbaum as Leo, Peggy Steffans as Leo's Vera, Jerome Raphel as Father, Blanche Dee as Mother, Ed Emshwiller as Gideon, Jerome Hill and Taylor Mead as the Convicts

Program V

Come Back, Africa
(1959)   84 minutes

Written, produced and directed by Lionel Rogosin
Cinematography: Ernst Artaria and Emil Knebel
Editor: Carl Lerner
Sound: Walter Wettler
Music editor: Lucy Brown
With: Lewis Nkosi, William Modisane, and featuring the people of Johannesburg, South Africa: Zacharia, Vinah, Arnold, Auntie, Dube-Dube, Eddy, George, Marumu, Miriam Makeba, Morris, Myrtle, Rams and Stevens

The Brig
(1964)   68 minutes

Photographed and filmically conceived by Jonas Mekas
Based on the play by Kenneth H. Brown as staged by Judith Malina and Julian Beck at The Living Theatre
Producer: David C. Stone
Editor: Adolfas Mekas
With: Warren Finnerty, Jim Anderson, Henry Howard, Tom Lillard, James Tiroff, Steven Ben Israel, Gene Lipton, Rufus Collins, Michael Elias, William Shari, Viktor Allen, George Bartenieff, Gene Gordon, Mark Duffy, Henry Proach, Carl Einhorn, Luke Theodore

Program VI

David Holzman's Diary
(1967)   73 minutes

A film by Jim McBride
Cinematography: Michael Wadleigh
Additional photography: Paul Goldsmith and Paul Glickman
With: L.M. Kit Carson as David Holzman, Penny Wohl, Lorenzo Mans, Louise Levine, Fern McBride, Michael Levine, Bob Lesser, Jack Baran

Portrait of Jason
(1967)   105 minutes

Director: Shirley Clarke
Assistant director: Jim Hubbard
Cinematography: Jeri Sapanen
Production assistant: Robert Fiore
Sound: Francis Daniel
With: Jason Holliday as Jason